THE LONG-TERM WILDERNESS SURVIVAL BIBLE [35 IN 1]

The Complete Guide to Make the Wild Your Safe Haven. Essential Skills to Build Shelter, Purify Water, Hunt for Food, and Navigate Without Tech

NATE COLTON

TABLE OF CONTENTS

INTRODUCTION

In today's uncertain world, the importance of wilderness survival has taken on new meaning. It's no longer just about adventuring or escaping into nature for a weekend getaway. Instead, it's about being prepared for situations where our modern systems might fail, leaving us to rely on the resources around us. Natural disasters are becoming more frequent, and social or economic instability can disrupt supply chains, leaving communities without access to essential supplies. In these scenarios, the skills to navigate, find food and water, build shelter, and maintain warmth are not just valuable—they can be life-saving. This guide is designed to transform the wilderness into a place of safety, equipping you with the skills to make the wild your sanctuary.

The guide's purpose is to take you through this transformation, not as a mere instruction manual, but as a comprehensive journey. It integrates practical skills with the psychological resilience needed for long-term wilderness living. You'll find that this guide is structured to help you not just survive, but thrive. How to Use This Guide Effectively is crucial for maximizing its value. This is not a traditional book that you simply read through. Instead, it is an interactive toolkit designed to be engaged with actively. Each section builds upon the last, progressing from foundational skills to more advanced techniques, ensuring that readers, regardless of experience level, can develop confidence and expertise step by step.

The book includes numerous practical exercises and self-assessment quizzes, encouraging readers to put what they've learned into practice. For example, when learning about fire-making techniques, you won't just read about them; you'll be prompted to gather the necessary materials and practice starting a fire using different methods. Whether it's the bow drill method or using flint and steel, the aim is for you to develop proficiency through hands-on experience. The guide challenges you to test these skills under varying conditions, such as in wet or windy environments, so that you'll have real-world practice before ever needing to rely on these abilities in a critical situation. This interactive approach ensures that each skill is internalized, allowing you to gain confidence gradually as you progress.

Another key aspect of this guide is its focus on mental resilience. The wilderness can be unpredictable, and without the right mindset, even the most physically prepared individuals can struggle. This book offers strategies for staying calm and focused under pressure, which is essential for long-term survival. Techniques such as deep breathing, visualization, and mindfulness are integrated into the survival framework, helping you manage stress and maintain clarity in high-stakes scenarios. Learning to cope with the challenges of fear, isolation, and uncertainty is just as important as mastering physical skills, and this guide emphasizes the development of both.

Physical preparation is equally important. The wilderness demands endurance and agility; tasks such as hiking through rough terrain, building shelters, or finding food require a certain level of physical readiness. This guide outlines fitness routines that can be easily incorporated into daily life, focusing on exercises that simulate real survival tasks. By building your strength and stamina over time, you will be better prepared for the physical challenges of the wilderness. The approach is designed to be accessible, ensuring that even those with limited time can gradually build the necessary fitness levels without needing a gym or specialized equipment.

Nutrition and diet are also emphasized as part of your preparation. To thrive in survival situations, it's essential to fuel your body correctly, both before and during your wilderness experience. The book explains how to optimize your diet for peak energy levels, focusing on foods that promote endurance and cognitive clarity. Additionally, it offers guidance on foraging, hunting, and preparing food once you're in the wild. Knowing how to identify edible plants, set up traps for small game, and cook with minimal tools are all skills that will be critical to maintaining your energy levels during extended periods in nature. The emphasis is not only on finding food but also on practicing sustainable techniques that minimize environmental impact, ensuring resources are available for future use.

The guide also addresses navigation without technology, an essential skill for wilderness survival. While modern devices are convenient, they are not always reliable in extended survival scenarios where batteries run out or networks fail. You'll learn to navigate using natural indicators like the sun, stars, and landmarks, as well as how to create simple tools such as improvised compasses. Developing these navigation skills will allow you to move confidently through unfamiliar terrain, turning the wilderness into a more navigable and less intimidating space. By understanding the landscape and learning how to read natural cues, you reduce reliance on technology and increase your sense of autonomy.

Another crucial element is the emphasis on sustainable interaction with the environment. While the guide covers techniques for foraging and hunting, it does so with a focus on sustainability. It emphasizes practices that are ethical and minimize harm to the ecosystem, ensuring that you can rely on the environment's resources for the long term. Learning to live harmoniously with nature not only enhances your survival capabilities but also fosters a deeper connection and respect for the wilderness as a living system.

Preparing Yourself Mentally and Physically for the Journey is about more than just acquiring skills; it's about cultivating a mindset and physical readiness that aligns with long-term wilderness living. Before you embark on this journey, it's essential to strengthen your mental and physical resilience. This guide provides the tools you need to develop these attributes, ensuring you are well-prepared for the challenges that lie ahead. It helps shift your perspective, enabling you to see the wilderness not as an obstacle but as a resource-rich environment where you can thrive independently.

The journey through this guide will transform your perception of the wilderness. Instead of seeing it as a place of fear or uncertainty, you'll begin to view it as a space where you can be self-sufficient, drawing from the land everything you need to live independently. This shift in perspective is crucial for anyone looking to thrive, not just survive, in nature.

This book is your comprehensive companion, designed to be taken with you into the field as a reference and a source of support. It's not just about what you know but how you apply that knowledge in real situations. Whether you are planning a long-term wilderness experience or simply want to be prepared for the unexpected, this guide will equip you with the skills, mindset, and confidence to make the wild your safe haven. Embrace this journey, and you will find that the skills you develop are not only valuable in the wilderness but also transferable to other aspects of your life, building resilience, resourcefulness, and independence that extend far beyond the confines of civilization.

BOOK 1
THE SURVIVOR MINDSET

UNDERSTANDING LONG-TERM WILDERNESS SURVIVAL

Wilderness survival is more than just an exercise in physical endurance; it is a test of mental strength, adaptability, and a deep understanding of how to live harmoniously with nature. In long-term wilderness survival situations, the stakes are higher, and the challenges are more demanding. It's not just about making it through a night in the woods—it's about learning how to establish a life that is sustainable over weeks, months, or even years. This perspective shift is crucial. To truly understand long-term survival, one must see beyond the immediate need for food, water, and shelter and begin to view the wilderness as a place where independence, creativity, and resilience merge to create a self-sufficient way of life.

The wilderness can be an intimidating and unforgiving environment. Without the proper mindset, even the most skilled individuals can find themselves overwhelmed by the sheer isolation and unpredictability of nature. To endure long-term survival, it is essential to approach the wilderness not as an enemy but as a complex system that offers everything needed to survive, if only you know how to access it. This requires developing a mindset that is not only resilient but also flexible enough to adapt to constantly changing conditions. It's about embracing the challenges that nature presents as opportunities for growth and learning, rather than obstacles.

Survival in the wilderness extends beyond knowing how to build a fire or forage for food. It involves a comprehensive understanding of natural cycles, such as weather patterns, wildlife behavior, and seasonal changes. Anticipating these shifts allows you to plan and act accordingly. For instance, understanding when and where animals are most active can influence hunting strategies, while knowing the signs of approaching storms can prompt quick adjustments to shelter and fire maintenance. Long-term survival isn't just about reacting to situations; it's about reading the environment and anticipating needs before they become urgent.

Furthermore, the wilderness demands a balance between assertiveness and patience. It's vital to take decisive actions—like securing a water source or constructing a shelter—when necessary. However, the ability to stay patient, observing your surroundings and adapting slowly, is just as important. Sometimes, rushing a task or acting impulsively can lead to mistakes that, in survival situations, may have severe consequences. Adopting a patient approach and taking the time to understand the terrain, observe wildlife, or test shelter stability can mean the difference between success and failure.

Ultimately, understanding long-term wilderness survival means preparing for the reality that it's not a sprint; it's a marathon. It's about creating a life in harmony with nature's rhythm rather than fighting against it. The skills you develop—whether they involve tracking animals, recognizing edible plants, or constructing advanced shelters—are only part of the equation. It is the mindset that binds these skills together, allowing you to maintain focus, manage resources wisely, and stay adaptable as conditions shift. This guide will explore the elements that contribute to cultivating this mindset, providing a strong foundation for anyone preparing for a long-term wilderness experience.

BUILDING MENTAL RESILIENCE AND MANAGING FEAR

The wilderness, despite its beauty and resources, can be a place of extreme stress. Being isolated and exposed to unpredictable elements requires not just physical skills but a high degree of mental resilience. In the face of fear and uncertainty, the ability to stay calm, focused, and rational is often what determines survival. Mental resilience isn't something that happens overnight; it's cultivated through practice, self-awareness, and strategic techniques that prepare you for the emotional and psychological demands of long-term wilderness survival.

Fear is a natural response to the unknown and can be a powerful tool when managed correctly. In survival scenarios, fear serves as a signal that something is amiss, prompting you to take necessary precautions. However, unmanaged fear can spiral into panic, clouding judgment and leading to poor decision-making. One of the most crucial skills in long-term survival is learning how to control and harness fear, using it as a motivator rather than allowing it to paralyze you. This involves developing techniques that center and ground you when anxiety rises.

One effective technique is deep breathing. When faced with a stressful or frightening situation, taking slow, deep breaths helps reduce the body's fight-or-flight response, calming the nervous system and allowing you to think clearly. Deep breathing, combined with visualization, where you picture a safe and successful outcome, can help reframe your perspective, turning fear into focused energy. Visualizing positive scenarios, such as safely navigating a challenging landscape or successfully lighting a fire in harsh conditions, builds confidence and mentally prepares you for the task at hand.

Another key aspect of building resilience is practicing mindfulness. Being fully present in the moment, rather than worrying about potential dangers or outcomes, allows you to focus on immediate tasks. This state of awareness is particularly useful in the wilderness, where distractions or inattention can lead to accidents or missed opportunities. Practicing mindfulness in daily life, such as through meditation or conscious breathing exercises, trains your mind to remain steady and attentive even in stressful situations.

In addition to controlling fear, long-term wilderness survival often involves managing loneliness. Isolation can have a profound psychological impact, making it crucial to find ways to stay mentally and emotionally engaged. One method is to establish routines. Creating a daily schedule that includes checking your shelter, collecting food, and practicing skills not only keeps you busy but also provides a sense of structure and normalcy. These routines anchor you, providing a consistent rhythm that counters the aimlessness and anxiety that isolation might provoke.

Another strategy is to engage in activities that foster a connection to nature. Observing wildlife, tracking animal behavior, or learning about plant species can give you a sense of purpose and place within the ecosystem. This engagement not only enriches your survival skills but also creates a sense of companionship, even in solitude. Over time, this bond with your environment can replace the feeling of loneliness with one of belonging, reinforcing mental resilience and providing comfort.

DEVELOPING A POSITIVE AND ADAPTABLE ATTITUDE

A positive and adaptable attitude is one of the most powerful tools in long-term wilderness survival. When faced with unpredictable and often harsh conditions, having the mental flexibility to adjust your plans and maintain a hopeful outlook becomes critical. The wilderness is dynamic—what works one day may not work the next. The ability to stay optimistic and adaptable ensures that you can navigate these changes effectively, finding solutions where others might see obstacles.

Maintaining a positive mindset doesn't mean ignoring the difficulties you encounter. It means recognizing challenges as opportunities for learning and growth. For example, if an attempt to build a shelter fails due to heavy rain or poor material choices, viewing this not as a setback but as a chance to refine your skills makes all the difference. This kind of perspective shift transforms mistakes into valuable lessons that prepare you for future situations. With each challenge you overcome, you build confidence, reinforcing the belief that you have the capacity to adapt and succeed.

An adaptable mindset involves not being overly attached to a single plan or strategy. In survival situations, conditions can change rapidly, requiring you to adjust your approach. For instance, if a planned water source dries up, the adaptable individual quickly seeks alternatives without hesitation, assessing the situation logically and taking immediate action. Cultivating this flexibility means practicing various skills and strategies in advance, so you have multiple options to draw upon when needed. It's about preparing not just for what you expect, but for the unexpected.

A key aspect of maintaining a positive and adaptable attitude is focusing on what you can control while accepting what you cannot. You may not be able to control the weather, but you can control how you respond to it—by preparing shelters, managing firewood, and maintaining your gear. By focusing on actions within your control, you create a sense of agency and empowerment, which is crucial in maintaining morale during difficult times.

Lastly, developing a sense of gratitude can significantly enhance your outlook. In the wilderness, small successes, like catching a fish or successfully starting a fire, can be celebrated as victories. Acknowledging these moments helps sustain a positive attitude, reminding you of the progress you've made and reinforcing the belief that you have the skills and mindset to thrive. Practicing gratitude, even for the simplest things—like a sunny day or a safe shelter—keeps your spirits high and your perspective grounded, no matter the challenges you face.

By cultivating a positive and adaptable attitude, you equip yourself with a mindset that can navigate the ups and downs of wilderness survival. It is this mindset, combined with resilience and the understanding of survival fundamentals, that forms the foundation for thriving in nature.

BOOK 2
PHYSICAL PREPARATION

FITNESS REGIMENS FOR ENDURANCE AND STRENGTH

Physical preparation is an essential aspect of long-term wilderness survival. While mental resilience and technical skills are crucial, your body must be capable of enduring the physical challenges that come with living in the wild for extended periods. The wilderness often demands hiking long distances, carrying heavy loads, constructing shelters, gathering resources, and sometimes climbing rough terrain—all of which require a solid foundation of physical fitness. Endurance and strength are not only advantageous; they are necessary for survival.

Building endurance is about preparing your body to sustain energy output over long periods. Wilderness survival often involves extended periods of physical exertion, sometimes with little rest in between. Therefore, it's important to focus on aerobic exercises like running, hiking, or cycling that gradually build cardiovascular strength and stamina. Start by incorporating long walks or hikes into your routine, gradually increasing the distance and intensity. If possible, practice hiking on varied terrains, such as hills and rough trails, to mimic the conditions you may face in the wild. By acclimating your body to these types of challenges, you'll improve your ability to traverse large areas efficiently while conserving energy.

Strength training is equally important in preparing for wilderness survival. Activities like lifting logs for firewood, building shelters, and carrying supplies all require physical strength. It's essential to focus on functional strength exercises—those that target muscle groups used in real-world activities. Bodyweight exercises such as squats, lunges, push-ups, and pull-ups are excellent for building overall strength without the need for gym equipment. These exercises can be done anywhere and prepare your body for the types of movements you'll need to perform in the wilderness.

Another effective approach is to incorporate circuit training, which combines strength and endurance exercises to simulate the physical demands of survival scenarios. A simple circuit might include a combination of squats, push-ups, and jumping jacks performed in sequence with minimal rest. This method not only builds strength but also enhances stamina, making it easier for you to maintain physical output over long durations. The goal is to create a regimen that improves your body's ability to handle high levels of activity with minimal recovery time, as wilderness conditions may not always provide opportunities for rest.

Training with weights or resistance bands is also beneficial, as it strengthens muscles used in lifting and carrying, both of which are common tasks in the wilderness. Focus on compound movements like deadlifts, rows, and presses, as they work multiple muscle groups at once, mirroring the functional strength required in survival situations. By progressively increasing the weight and intensity of these exercises, you build the muscle endurance and power needed for long-term physical demands. Remember, the goal is to build a balanced physique that combines both power and stamina, enabling you to manage the varied and often intense physical challenges of wilderness life.

FUNCTIONAL EXERCISES FOR WILDERNESS READINESS

Fitness regimens designed specifically for wilderness readiness focus on functional exercises—movements that mimic real tasks you are likely to encounter in survival situations. Unlike traditional gym workouts, which often isolate muscle groups, functional exercises engage multiple muscles at once, promoting coordination, balance, and strength. This holistic approach ensures that your body is well-prepared for the diverse physical tasks required when navigating and surviving in nature.

One of the most beneficial exercises for wilderness preparedness is the loaded carry. This movement involves walking or hiking while carrying a heavy object, such as a weighted backpack or log. This simulates the need to transport supplies, firewood, or equipment over long distances. Practicing loaded carries strengthens your core, back, shoulders, and legs, improving your ability to maintain balance and control under weight. To make this exercise more effective, vary the weight and the terrain, training on hills, uneven paths, or rocky surfaces to mirror real wilderness conditions.

Another crucial exercise is the lunge, which builds lower body strength and stability. In survival situations, you may need to traverse rough terrain, climb steep slopes, or maneuver through dense vegetation. Lunges train your body to remain stable in these situations, enhancing balance and building leg strength. For added benefit, incorporate lunges with a twist, holding a weighted object in your hands and twisting your torso as you lunge. This adds a rotational element, simulating the movements needed when chopping wood, clearing debris, or setting up camp.

The plank and its variations are also excellent for wilderness readiness, as they engage the entire core, shoulders, and back muscles. A strong core is essential for stability when lifting, carrying, or pulling objects, all of which are common survival tasks. Planking also improves posture and balance, which are critical when moving through uneven or challenging landscapes. Variations like side planks or plank rows introduce more complexity, working on different muscle groups and further developing functional strength.

Incorporating agility exercises is another key aspect of wilderness fitness. The ability to move quickly and efficiently, particularly through dense forests or rocky paths, can make a significant difference in your ability to escape dangerous situations or travel between locations. Agility drills, such as ladder exercises, box jumps, or cone drills, improve your speed and coordination. These exercises simulate the quick changes in direction and bursts of speed that might be needed when navigating obstacles or moving quickly in response to wildlife encounters.

Balance and flexibility exercises, like yoga or balance beam walks, also contribute to wilderness readiness. Yoga, in particular, is beneficial because it enhances flexibility, reduces injury risk, and improves mental focus, all of which are crucial in survival scenarios. Balancing exercises improve your stability on uneven terrain, helping you traverse tricky landscapes without falling or injuring yourself. Flexibility and balance ensure that your body remains adaptable, reducing strain and allowing for greater range of motion when reaching for branches, climbing, or navigating difficult paths.

By combining these functional exercises into your fitness routine, you prepare your body for the dynamic, unpredictable conditions of the wilderness. Training with purpose and intention not only builds physical strength but also develops the coordination, balance, and endurance necessary for long-term survival. Regularly practicing these movements, both with and without added weight or resistance, ensures that you build a body capable of adapting and performing when faced with real-world challenges.

DIETARY PREPARATION FOR SUSTAINED ENERGY

Physical fitness alone is not sufficient for wilderness survival; nutrition plays an equally critical role. What you consume before and during your time in the wilderness has a direct impact on your physical performance, energy levels, and overall health. Preparing your body nutritionally ensures that you can endure the strenuous physical activities required for survival while maintaining mental clarity and stamina.

Before heading into the wilderness, it is important to adopt a diet that builds your endurance and strength over time. Focusing on nutrient-dense foods that provide long-lasting energy, such as complex carbohydrates, lean proteins, and healthy fats, is key. Whole grains like quinoa, oats, and brown rice offer sustained energy release, while lean proteins such as chicken, fish, and plant-based options like lentils and beans help build and repair muscle tissue. Healthy fats found in nuts, seeds, and avocados provide essential energy reserves that your body can draw upon during extended periods of exertion.

Hydration is also a critical component of dietary preparation. Drinking plenty of water and consuming foods with high water content, such as fruits and vegetables, ensures that your body stays hydrated and your muscles perform optimally. Proper hydration supports muscle function, prevents fatigue, and helps maintain mental clarity—all essential for survival situations where physical and cognitive demands are high. In addition to water, electrolyte-rich drinks or foods like coconut water or bananas can help maintain electrolyte balance, which is important when engaging in prolonged physical activities.

During your wilderness experience, finding and maintaining energy sources becomes paramount. Understanding how to forage for nutrient-rich plants, catch small game, and preserve food ensures that you sustain energy levels while minimizing environmental impact. Learning to recognize and safely consume edible plants, berries, and insects provides access to critical nutrients when other food sources are scarce. The guide details methods for preparing these foods, maximizing their nutritional value while ensuring they are safe to eat.

Fats and proteins become especially important in long-term survival situations, as they offer more energy per gram than carbohydrates and help sustain you through longer periods without food. Nuts, seeds, and dried meats (such as jerky) are excellent sources of energy that can be carried easily and eaten on the go. Incorporating fishing or trapping into your survival skills not only provides high-protein options like fish or small mammals but also diversifies your diet, helping to maintain energy levels and physical strength.

Cooking methods that retain nutrients, such as boiling or steaming, are also vital to maintaining a nutritious diet in the wilderness. This guide explores how to create cooking setups using minimal resources, such as using heated stones or building an earth oven. These techniques ensure that you can prepare food in ways that maximize its energy value, fueling your body efficiently. The ability to dry or smoke meats and fish is another key skill, allowing for long-term food storage that provides consistent nutrition over time.

Adapting your body to a nutrient-rich, balanced diet before you embark on your wilderness journey makes the transition to survival foods smoother. By training your body to rely on whole foods and complex nutrients rather than processed options, you build a more resilient system capable of thriving on the resources found in nature. It's about conditioning your body not just through physical training but through thoughtful nutrition that supports your long-term energy and health needs.

Preparing physically for wilderness survival is not only about building strength and endurance; it's also about ensuring your body is fueled properly, so it functions efficiently in all conditions. By combining a fitness regimen that builds the necessary strength and stamina with a diet that sustains energy and health, you create a well-rounded foundation for long-term survival. This preparation gives you the confidence to face wilderness challenges, knowing that your body is capable and ready for whatever nature presents.

BOOK 3
SHELTER BUILDING BASICS

Shelter is one of the most critical elements of wilderness survival. Without proper protection from the elements, exposure to extreme weather conditions—such as cold, heat, rain, or wind—can quickly become life-threatening. Knowing how to build a reliable shelter using natural materials not only helps regulate body temperature but also provides a sense of security and comfort, both of which are essential for maintaining mental resilience. This chapter focuses on the fundamentals of shelter building, emphasizing basic techniques that can be used with minimal tools and resources. From constructing a simple debris hut to building an insulated lean-to, these foundational shelters are designed to provide the protection you need in various environments. Additionally, understanding common shelter issues and their solutions ensures that you can adapt and troubleshoot effectively when conditions change.

CONSTRUCTING A DEBRIS HUT FROM NATURAL MATERIALS

The debris hut is one of the simplest and most effective shelters to construct in the wilderness. It uses natural materials like branches, leaves, and moss, making it an ideal option when tools or equipment are limited. The design of the debris hut is focused on maximizing insulation by using layers of organic material to trap body heat, ensuring warmth even in cold conditions. This shelter type is versatile and can be adapted based on available resources and weather conditions.

Steps for Constructing a Debris Hut:

1. Find a Suitable Location:

- Choose a spot that is slightly elevated and away from water sources to prevent flooding in case of rain.

- Look for a location near abundant resources like fallen branches, leaves, and other organic matter.

2. Set Up the Ridgepole:

- Locate a sturdy branch or log to serve as the central support (ridgepole). This should be long enough to create the length of your shelter.

- Secure one end of the ridgepole against a stable base like a tree stump, rock, or Y-shaped branch, keeping the other end on the ground.

3. Construct the Framework:

- Lean smaller branches (ribs) against the ridgepole at an angle, creating a triangular structure. Ensure the ribs are close enough to provide support but leave small gaps for airflow.

4. Add Insulation:

- Pile leaves, moss, and other natural debris over the framework. The thicker the layer, the better the insulation. Aim for at least 1-2 feet of material to trap body heat effectively.
- Cover the entrance partially to retain warmth while allowing room for entry and exit.

Benefits of a Debris Hut:

- Thermal efficiency: The thick insulation helps maintain body heat, making it an ideal option for cold environments.
- Ease of construction: Requires minimal resources and can be built quickly, which is crucial when daylight or energy levels are limited.

Considerations:

- Make sure the materials are dry to avoid dampness, which can lower the insulation value and lead to discomfort or hypothermia.
- Check for stability before fully settling inside to prevent collapse, particularly if the shelter is built with heavy branches.

BUILDING AN INSULATED LEAN-TO FOR PROTECTION

While the debris hut is effective for cold weather, the lean-to shelter is another versatile option that works well in a variety of climates. Unlike the debris hut, which encloses the body entirely, the lean-to is an open-fronted structure, ideal for situations where you need a quick shelter or need to keep an eye on your surroundings. The lean-to provides protection from the wind, rain, and sun, while also being suitable for building a fire directly in front of it for warmth.

Steps for Building an Insulated Lean-To:

1. Find a Sturdy Support:

- Look for two strong trees or supports close together (about 6-8 feet apart) to anchor your ridgepole. Alternatively, use a large log or rock if trees are not available.

2. Set the Ridgepole:

- Secure the ridgepole horizontally between the supports at a height that allows you to sit or lie comfortably under the lean-to. Ensure it is stable and won't move under the weight of the structure.

3. Add Ribs and Insulation:

- Lean branches at an angle against the ridgepole, forming the back wall of the lean-to. Cover these branches with a thick layer of leaves, ferns, or other insulating material. Add additional branches and debris to create a dense layer that blocks wind and retains heat.

4. Create a Fire Reflector:

- Build a small wall of logs or rocks directly in front of the lean-to to reflect heat from a fire back into the shelter. This not only provides warmth but also improves the shelter's thermal efficiency by trapping heat.

Advantages of a Lean-To:

- Provides quick and effective protection from wind and rain.
- Works well in combination with a fire for warmth, as the open front allows heat to enter directly.
- Allows visibility and monitoring of the surroundings, which is important for safety.

Potential Challenges:

- The open design means that it may not be suitable for extreme cold without the addition of a heat source, such as a fire.
- If not properly insulated, it may not retain enough warmth, especially in wet or windy conditions.

TROUBLESHOOTING COMMON SHELTER ISSUES

No shelter is perfect, and in the wilderness, unforeseen issues are likely to arise. Understanding common shelter problems and how to address them is a crucial skill that can prevent discomfort and enhance your chances of staying safe and warm.

1. Shelter Instability:

- If the structure collapses or shifts, it's likely due to an inadequate ridgepole or poorly anchored ribs. Ensure that the ridgepole is securely placed against a stable support and that ribs are anchored at a strong angle.
- In windy conditions, add weight to the base of the ribs using rocks or heavy logs. This will stabilize the structure and prevent it from being blown over.

2. Poor Insulation:

- If the shelter fails to retain heat, it may not have enough insulating material. Add extra layers of leaves, ferns, or moss to increase the thickness. A good rule of thumb is that the insulation should be thick enough to prevent light from passing through when viewed from the inside.
- If dry materials are not available, use branches with dense foliage to create an initial layer, then add whatever insulation you can find.

3. Dampness and Moisture:

- If the shelter becomes damp or wet, it can lower the insulation value and lead to hypothermia. Ensure that the shelter is built on slightly elevated ground to avoid water pooling. If available, line the floor with dry leaves or branches to create a barrier between you and the ground.

- In rainy conditions, create an overhang at the entrance of the shelter using additional branches and leaves to divert water away from the interior.

4. Wind Exposure:

- Wind can penetrate a shelter that isn't properly oriented or insulated. Position your shelter with its back to the prevailing wind, using natural windbreaks like large rocks or tree clusters when possible.

- Reinforce the back of the shelter with thick layers of debris to reduce wind chill and prevent drafts.

By understanding these common issues and implementing simple solutions, you can ensure that your shelter remains effective and comfortable. Practice building different types of shelters in various conditions to develop the skills and confidence needed to quickly adapt and respond when facing real survival situations. This knowledge forms a solid foundation for shelter building, enabling you to establish reliable protection regardless of the environment or available resources.

BOOK 4
ADVANCED SHELTER TECHNIQUES

When surviving long-term in the wilderness, a simple shelter may suffice for a night or two, but extended stays require a more robust and sustainable approach. For individuals planning to live in the wilderness for weeks, months, or even years, knowing how to build advanced shelters that can accommodate groups, withstand harsh weather, and be easily reinforced using natural materials is essential. This chapter focuses on crafting group shelters that provide stability and durability, using natural resources to strengthen your shelter, and weatherproofing and insulating large structures to create a comfortable living space even in the most challenging environments.

CRAFTING GROUP SHELTERS FOR LONG-TERM LIVING

When planning to survive long-term, particularly with a group or family, a more expansive and stable shelter becomes a necessity. A group shelter must accommodate multiple people and provide space for sleeping, storage, and daily activities like cooking. The shelter's design should also allow for flexibility to be expanded or modified as needs change. This section explores three types of group shelters suitable for long-term wilderness living: the longhouse, the tarp cabin, and the A-frame log shelter.

1. The Longhouse:

*   The longhouse is one of the most traditional types of group shelters, used by indigenous communities for centuries. Its elongated shape provides ample space for multiple occupants and allows for internal divisions, making it ideal for family or group survival scenarios.

*   To build a longhouse, begin by selecting a location with abundant resources, such as a wooded area with plenty of logs and leaves. Clear the ground of debris and level it as much as possible. Start by placing two parallel logs on the ground as the foundation. These logs should be as long as you want your shelter to be and as straight as possible.

*   Erect the walls using upright posts (about 6-8 feet apart) along the length of the foundation logs. Lash horizontal beams across the tops of these posts using cordage made from vines, roots, or bark. Once the frame is secure, fill the gaps with smaller logs, branches, and woven saplings.

*   The roof is the most critical part of the longhouse, as it provides the bulk of the insulation and weatherproofing. Construct a thatched roof using layers of leaves, grass, and bark, tightly packed to prevent leaks. The roof should slope downward to direct rainwater away from the structure. Ensure that the walls are reinforced with mud or clay for additional insulation, especially in colder climates.

*   Advantages:

- » The longhouse can accommodate multiple people, making it ideal for group survival.
  - » The structure is easily expandable, allowing you to adjust the size as needed.

- Considerations:
  - » Building a longhouse requires time and a significant amount of resources, so it is best suited for areas with abundant materials and stable weather conditions during construction.

2. The Tarp Cabin:

- The tarp cabin combines simplicity and flexibility, using tarps as the main roofing material while integrating natural resources for the walls and frame. This shelter is particularly useful when you have access to durable tarps or large pieces of fabric but still want a semi-permanent structure.

- To construct a tarp cabin, start by building a basic A-frame structure using logs or poles. The frame should be tall enough to stand inside and long enough to accommodate sleeping spaces for multiple people. Secure the frame with strong lashing or rope, ensuring that it is stable.

- Lay the tarp over the A-frame, ensuring it is tightly secured and extends down both sides to the ground. Use stakes or additional logs to anchor the tarp, preventing it from flapping in the wind. For the walls, use a combination of logs, branches, and woven saplings to create a barrier that insulates and protects the interior. Cover the floor with leaves, moss, or other natural insulation to provide comfort and warmth.

- The tarp cabin can be modified with additional tarps or sections of fabric to create enclosed rooms or additional storage spaces.

- Advantages:
  - » The tarp cabin is faster to build than other group shelters and can be set up or taken down relatively quickly.
  - » It offers a blend of portability and stability, making it suitable for situations where you may need to relocate your shelter.

- Considerations:
  - » The tarp cabin's durability depends heavily on the quality of the tarp material. Regular maintenance is necessary to ensure that the tarp remains waterproof and secure.

3. The A-Frame Log Shelter:

- The A-frame log shelter is a solid and durable option for long-term living, particularly in wooded areas where logs are abundant. This type of shelter is excellent for withstanding heavy snow or rain, as its steeply sloped roof allows precipitation to run off efficiently.

- Begin by finding two long logs of equal length for the base. These logs will act as the foundation. Dig shallow trenches and place the logs parallel to each other, then set upright support beams at the ends and center. Lash a ridgepole between the supports, creating the frame for the roof.

- Build the walls using logs of varying sizes, stacking them horizontally and securing them with notches or lashings. Ensure that the roof slope is steep enough to shed rain and snow. For the roof covering, use branches, bark, and leaves, layering them to create a thick, insulated barrier. If clay or mud is available, apply it to the walls for added insulation.

- Advantages:

  » The A-frame log shelter is incredibly sturdy, making it ideal for harsh climates.
  » It offers a semi-permanent solution that can last through multiple seasons if properly maintained.

- Considerations:

  » Construction requires significant labor and time, as well as a good selection of logs and lashings. It is best built with a team to speed up the process.

USING NATURAL RESOURCES FOR REINFORCEMENT

In long-term survival scenarios, maintaining and reinforcing your shelter is vital for ensuring safety and comfort over time. Using natural resources for reinforcement not only enhances the durability of your shelter but also allows you to make use of the materials around you, conserving energy and avoiding reliance on artificial or limited supplies.

1. Cordage:

- Natural cordage is one of the most valuable resources for shelter reinforcement. It can be made from a variety of plant materials such as vines, tree bark, grasses, or even roots. When woven tightly, cordage provides a strong binding agent for securing logs, beams, and other shelter components.

- To make cordage, choose fibrous plants like cattails, nettles, or willow bark. Strip the fibers and twist them together, gradually adding more strands for strength. Practice making cordage in different thicknesses, as some parts of the shelter may need thicker bindings (e.g., ridgepoles) while others (e.g., walls) may require thinner, more flexible lashings.

2. Clay and Mud:

- For additional insulation and weatherproofing, clay and mud can be used as a natural sealant for shelters. Applying clay to the walls of a log or longhouse shelter creates a solid barrier that prevents drafts and keeps heat trapped inside. In colder environments, clay acts as a thermal mass, absorbing and slowly releasing heat throughout the day and night.

- When using clay, ensure it is well-mixed with straw or plant fibers to improve its adhesive properties and prevent cracking as it dries. Apply the clay in layers, allowing each to dry partially before adding the next. This method increases the structural strength and longevity of the shelter.

3. Thatch and Leaves:

- A thick layer of thatch—composed of grasses, leaves, or reeds—can provide an excellent natural roof covering. Thatching helps shed rain and provides additional insulation, keeping the interior of the shelter warm in winter and cool in summer. When creating a thatched roof, start at the bottom and work your way up, overlapping each layer like shingles to ensure water runs off without penetrating the shelter.

- Collecting large leaves, such as those from palms or ferns, can also be used for thatching. Lay these leaves in layers, securing them with branches or cordage to prevent them from shifting in strong winds.

WEATHERPROOFING AND INSULATING LARGE SHELTERS

In long-term wilderness survival, protecting your shelter against weather extremes—such as heavy rain, snow, or intense heat—is critical for maintaining a safe living environment. Proper weatherproofing and insulation techniques can mean the difference between comfort and exposure, particularly in harsh climates.

1. Waterproofing with Natural Materials:

- Rain poses a significant threat to shelter integrity, and keeping the interior dry is essential for comfort and health. A waterproof barrier can be created using bark from trees such as birch or cedar, which naturally repels water. Lay the bark in overlapping layers on the roof and secure it with cordage or additional branches to prevent leaks.

- Another effective technique is to dig drainage ditches around the shelter's perimeter. These ditches direct rainwater away from the structure, preventing water from pooling and seeping into the ground underneath.

2. Insulating for Cold Weather:

- Insulation is particularly important for maintaining warmth during cold months. In addition to building thick walls, applying natural insulation such as moss, pine needles, or leaves between layers of logs can significantly improve thermal retention. The compacted layers trap air, creating a barrier against cold winds.

- Double-layering walls with an air gap in between is another method to improve insulation. This technique is similar to modern double-pane windows, where the air trapped between the layers acts as an insulator. Fill the gap with leaves, dried grass, or other natural material for extra effectiveness.

3. Protection Against Heat:

- In hot climates, shelters need to be ventilated and shaded to maintain a comfortable temperature. Use large leaves or woven mats to create shade extensions over the shelter, reducing direct sunlight exposure. Elevate the shelter floor if possible, using logs or stones, to allow airflow underneath and prevent heat buildup.

- Position the shelter to take advantage of natural breezes, ensuring that ventilation holes are placed in strategic locations to allow air to flow through. Light-colored materials, such as pale leaves or grass, can also be used for roofing to reflect rather than absorb heat.

TIPS FOR MAINTAINING LONG-TERM SHELTERS

Ensuring your shelter remains functional over an extended period requires regular maintenance and adaptation. Here are some key tips for keeping your shelter in top condition:

- Check for Leaks: After heavy rain, inspect the roof for any leaks and reinforce with additional thatch or bark if needed. Patch holes immediately to prevent further damage.

- Reinforce Structural Components: Examine load-bearing parts of the shelter, such as ridgepoles and support beams, for signs of wear or instability. Replace or reinforce these components with new logs or thicker lashings.

- Seasonal Adjustments: Adapt the shelter for seasonal changes—adding extra insulation as winter approaches or increasing ventilation as temperatures rise. Small adjustments can greatly enhance comfort and safety.

CONCLUSION

Advanced shelter techniques are essential for those planning to survive long-term in the wilderness, especially with a group. By learning how to craft robust shelters like the longhouse or A-frame log shelter, utilize natural resources for reinforcement, and effectively weatherproof and insulate large structures, you create a secure living space that can sustain you and your group through changing conditions. Mastering these skills not only increases your chances of survival but also provides the foundation for a more comfortable and resilient wilderness experience.

BOOK 5
FIRE-STARTING TECHNIQUES

Fire is one of the most fundamental elements of survival in the wilderness. It provides warmth, allows you to cook food, purify water, signal for help, and create light. Knowing how to start a fire in different conditions is a critical skill for long-term survival. This chapter focuses on mastering essential fire-starting techniques that do not rely on modern tools like lighters or matches, making it possible to create fire using natural or minimal resources. The key methods covered include mastering the bow drill, using flint and steel effectively, and fire-building in wet or rainy conditions. These techniques are essential for anyone seeking to be self-sufficient in the wilderness.

MASTERING THE BOW DRILL METHOD

The bow drill is one of the oldest and most reliable methods of starting a fire without modern tools. It relies solely on friction to generate heat, which then produces an ember that can be used to ignite tinder. While it may take practice to master, the bow drill is an invaluable skill that can be applied in almost any environment, as long as you have the basic materials.

Components of a Bow Drill:

- Bow: The bow is a curved stick with a cord attached at both ends. This cord (which can be made from shoelaces, paracord, or even natural fibers) wraps around the spindle, allowing you to create a sawing motion.
- Spindle: The spindle is a straight, dry piece of wood that rotates against the fireboard. It should be about 6-8 inches long and roughly the thickness of your thumb.
- Fireboard: This is a flat piece of wood with a depression where the spindle will rotate. The fireboard should be made of softwood like cedar, willow, or cottonwood for the best results.
- Handhold: A small, smooth piece of wood or stone that you can grip while pressing down on the spindle. It should be easy to hold and ideally fit comfortably in your hand to minimize friction.

Steps to Start a Fire with a Bow Drill:

1. Prepare the Fireboard:

- Create a small depression (also called a divot) in the fireboard where the spindle will sit.

Carve a V-shaped notch next to the depression. This notch will collect the ember created by the friction.

2. Assemble the Bow Drill:

- Wrap the bow's cord around the spindle once. The spindle should be positioned upright with one end in the fireboard's depression and the other supported by the handhold.

3. Create Friction:

- Hold the fireboard down with one foot, pressing it against the ground for stability. Apply downward pressure with the handhold, and move the bow back and forth in a sawing motion. This rotates the spindle rapidly against the fireboard, generating heat.

4. Form the Ember:

- Continue the sawing motion until smoke appears. Maintain steady pressure and speed until you see a small, glowing ember form in the fireboard's notch. This may take several minutes, so be patient and consistent.

5. Transfer the Ember:

- Carefully tap the fireboard to transfer the ember into a nest of dry tinder (e.g., grass, dry leaves, or wood shavings). Gently blow on the ember to ignite the tinder.

Tips for Success:

- Ensure that all materials are dry; moisture will make it much harder to create an ember.
- Choose softwood for the spindle and fireboard, as they generate friction more easily.
- Practice maintaining a consistent rhythm with the bow. Speed and pressure must be balanced to generate enough heat without exhausting yourself.

USING FLINT AND STEEL EFFECTIVELY

The flint and steel method is another traditional and reliable way to start a fire, especially when you have access to these materials. This technique is effective because it uses the spark created when striking steel against flint to ignite a piece of tinder, typically char cloth or another highly combustible material. With practice, this method can become a quick and dependable way to build a fire, even in challenging conditions.

Materials Needed:

- Flint: A hard rock that, when struck, produces a spark. Flint, chert, or quartz can be used for this purpose.
- Steel Striker: A piece of high-carbon steel. The striker can be a purpose-made fire steel, a knife blade, or any steel tool.
- Tinder: The most effective tinder for flint and steel is char cloth, a piece of fabric that has been heated without oxygen. Other options include fine wood shavings, dry grass, or cotton.

Steps to Start a Fire with Flint and Steel:

1. Prepare the Tinder:

• Make sure your tinder is dry and finely shredded to catch a spark easily. Place a small amount of tinder on top of the flint.

2. Hold the Flint and Striker:

• Hold the flint in one hand and the steel striker in the other. Angle the flint so that the edge faces up, with the tinder positioned close to where the spark will land.

3. Strike the Flint:

• Using the steel, strike downward against the flint at a sharp angle. The steel should scrape along the flint, generating sparks. Aim the sparks to land directly on the tinder.

4. Ignite the Tinder:

• Once a spark catches on the tinder, gently blow on it to increase the flame. Gradually add more tinder and small sticks to build the fire.

Advantages:

• Flint and steel are durable and can be used repeatedly, making them ideal for long-term survival scenarios.

• Once practiced, this method is fast and efficient, especially when dry materials are available.

Considerations:

• Practice is key. Striking the flint at the right angle and generating enough force takes skill.

• Having properly prepared tinder, like char cloth, significantly increases the success rate.

FIRE-BUILDING IN WET OR RAINY CONDITIONS

Fire-building in wet or rainy conditions is one of the greatest challenges in wilderness survival. Wet wood, damp tinder, and cold conditions can make it extremely difficult to start a fire, but there are techniques and strategies that can significantly increase your chances of success.

Finding and Preparing Dry Materials:

• Look Under Shelter: In rainy conditions, look for dry tinder and kindling underneath fallen logs, inside tree hollows, or under dense foliage. These areas are often sheltered from rain and may contain dry leaves, moss, or pine needles.

• Collect Small Branches: Even if it's raining, small dead branches found off the ground or hanging on trees may remain dry enough to use as kindling. Break off these branches and peel away the outer bark to expose the dry wood inside.

• Feather Sticks: When larger logs are damp, you can create feather sticks by shaving off the wet outer layer and whittling the dry inner wood into thin curls. These shavings catch fire more easily and burn longer, even when exposed to some moisture.

Techniques for Building a Fire in Wet Conditions:

1. Build a Platform:

*   To keep your fire off the wet ground, create a platform using dry branches, rocks, or bark. This prevents the fire from absorbing moisture and helps it burn more effectively.

2. Use a Reflective Barrier:

*   In wet or windy conditions, building a reflective barrier behind the fire helps concentrate heat and protect the flame. This barrier can be made from logs or stones arranged vertically behind the fire pit.

3. Layer Your Fire:

*   Start with the driest tinder you can find (such as feather sticks or fine shavings). Build a teepee structure using small, dry twigs and gradually add larger pieces as the fire grows stronger. Keep your fuel wood close to the fire to help it dry out as you continue to build the fire.

Using Specialized Techniques:

*   Fire Starters: In wet conditions, using a fire starter like birch bark (which burns even when wet) or resinous wood (fatwood) can be extremely helpful. These natural materials are excellent for igniting and sustaining a flame.
*   Improvised Windbreak: Create a temporary windbreak using tarps, branches, or your own body to shield the fire from rain and wind until it gains strength.

PRACTICING FIRE-BUILDING SKILLS

Fire-building is not just about knowing techniques but developing the skill to adapt those techniques to different conditions. Practicing in varied environments, such as after a rainstorm or during high humidity, builds confidence and skill. Here are some practical exercises to enhance your fire-building abilities:

1. Practice in Diverse Weather: Challenge yourself to build a fire in conditions you are less comfortable with, such as after rain or in high winds. This practice helps you identify suitable materials and refine your techniques under realistic conditions.
2. Test Different Materials: Try using different types of tinder and kindling, including pine needles, grass, and tree bark, to see what works best in various situations. Knowing what burns quickly and what requires more effort is essential.
3. Use Minimal Tools: Practice building fires using natural materials and traditional methods like the bow drill and flint and steel. Familiarity with these tools ensures that you can rely on them when other options are unavailable.

CONCLUSION

Mastering fire-starting techniques is a critical aspect of long-term wilderness survival. Whether you're using the ancient method of a bow drill, the reliable flint and steel, or adapting to wet conditions, being proficient in creating fire ensures warmth, safety, and comfort. By practicing these techniques and understanding how to adapt to challenging environments, you develop not only skill but confidence—an essential asset when facing the uncertainties of nature.

BOOK 6

WATER PURIFICATION METHODS

Water is one of the most crucial elements for survival in the wilderness. While the human body can survive weeks without food, it can only go a few days without water. Accessing and purifying water in the wild is a critical skill that must be mastered for long-term survival. Drinking contaminated water can lead to severe illnesses, such as bacterial infections, parasites, and dehydration, all of which can quickly become life-threatening. This chapter focuses on locating and accessing safe water sources, using natural filters for purification, and employing solar distillation and other improvised methods. Understanding and mastering these techniques will ensure that you can find and purify water effectively in various environments, safeguarding your health and survival.

LOCATING AND ACCESSING SAFE WATER SOURCES

Finding water in the wilderness requires knowledge and observational skills. While water is often present in the environment, it is not always visible or easily accessible. Streams, rivers, lakes, and ponds are the most obvious sources, but in a survival situation, knowing how to find less apparent water sources can be life-saving. Understanding the terrain, recognizing signs of water, and being aware of environmental cues are essential skills.

One of the best ways to locate water is to observe natural land formations. Valleys, ravines, and depressions in the landscape are likely places where water accumulates. Water naturally flows downhill, so following a downward slope or a dry creek bed can often lead to a water source. In arid regions, dry riverbeds may still contain water below the surface. Digging into the sand or soil of these areas may reveal underground water, though it is crucial to filter and purify this water before consumption.

Another key indicator of water is vegetation. Lush, green areas in an otherwise dry environment often indicate the presence of a water source. Plants like willows, reeds, and cattails thrive in moist soil, suggesting nearby water, even if it is underground. By digging near the base of these plants, it may be possible to access water through shallow wells. Animal tracks are also a helpful sign. Animals, particularly birds, tend to gather around water sources. Following their paths may lead you to water.

Morning dew is another valuable source, especially in arid environments where larger bodies of water may be scarce. By using a cloth or your hands to collect dew from grass and leaves early in the morning, you can gather small amounts of water. While it may not be sufficient for long-term hydration, it can help in a pinch.

In mountainous or forested regions, natural springs can provide clean water. Springs occur when groundwater rises to the surface, often resulting in clear, running water. These sources are typically cleaner than stagnant pools, but purification is still recommended. Springs are frequently found at the base of hills or near rock formations, where pressure forces water to the surface.

Rainwater is another critical source of hydration, particularly in tropical or temperate environments. When rain is expected, setting up collection systems with tarps, leaves, or even clothing can help gather large quantities of water. While rainwater is generally safe, collecting it directly in a clean container minimizes contamination from surfaces that might carry bacteria or pollutants.

By understanding these techniques for locating water, you gain an essential survival advantage. However, finding water is only the first step. Knowing how to purify it effectively is equally important to prevent illness and ensure safety.

PURIFICATION TECHNIQUES WITH NATURAL FILTERS

Even when water appears clean, it can harbor microorganisms, bacteria, and parasites that are invisible to the naked eye. Drinking untreated water can lead to serious health issues like giardia, dysentery, or other infections. Natural filtration methods, when properly executed, can significantly reduce these risks. These techniques use resources available in the wilderness, such as sand, charcoal, and gravel, to create effective, improvised filters.

Building a Simple Sand and Charcoal Filter: The sand and charcoal filter is one of the most reliable methods for purifying water in the wild. It mimics the filtration process of modern water filters but uses natural elements readily available in most environments. To construct this filter, you will need layers of materials, including sand, charcoal (if available), small pebbles, and grass or cloth to serve as a pre-filter.

1. Prepare the Materials: Gather fine sand, small pebbles or gravel, and charcoal (if you have access to a fire). Charcoal is particularly effective because its porous structure absorbs impurities and bacteria.
2. Layer the Filter:

- Start with a container, such as a plastic bottle with the bottom cut off or a hollowed-out log.
- Place a piece of cloth, grass, or large leaves at the bottom of the container to act as the initial filter layer.
- Add a layer of small pebbles, followed by a layer of charcoal.
- On top of the charcoal, add a layer of sand, followed by another layer of smaller pebbles. This multi-layer system ensures that larger debris is filtered first, with finer sand and charcoal catching smaller particles and microorganisms.

3. Filtering Process: Pour the collected water through the filter slowly, allowing it to trickle through each layer. This process removes sediments, larger particles, and some bacteria. Collect the water that comes out of the bottom and repeat the filtration process multiple times for the best results.

While this method is effective at removing visible impurities and some bacteria, it is essential to remember that it may not eliminate all pathogens. Therefore, combining filtration with boiling the filtered water is recommended to ensure complete purification.

USING SOLAR DISTILLATION AND IMPROVISED METHODS

When traditional methods like boiling are not possible—perhaps due to a lack of firewood or tools—other purification techniques can be employed. One such method is solar distillation, which uses the sun's heat to purify water by evaporation and condensation. This technique can be used to desalinate seawater, purify muddy or contaminated sources, and even collect water from vegetation.

Constructing a Solar Still

A solar still is an efficient way to purify water using minimal resources. It works by trapping moisture from the ground, vegetation, or other sources and condensing it into clean, drinkable water. To build a solar still:

1. Dig a Pit: Choose a location that receives plenty of sunlight throughout the day. Dig a pit about 3-4 feet wide and 1-2 feet deep. The depth may vary based on the soil type and available materials.
2. Add Greenery and a Container: Place fresh green plants and leaves inside the pit. These plants release moisture as they are exposed to the sun's heat. At the center of the pit, place a small container (such as a cup or bowl) where the purified water will collect.
3. Cover with Plastic: Stretch a clear plastic sheet over the pit, securing it with rocks or soil around the edges to create a seal. Weigh down the center of the plastic with a small rock, so it forms a cone shape, with the lowest point directly above the container.
4. Condensation and Collection: As the sun heats the pit, moisture from the soil and plants evaporates and condenses on the underside of the plastic sheet. The condensation will drip down to the lowest point, collecting in the container. This method can produce enough water to sustain you throughout the day, but multiple stills may be necessary for larger quantities.

Advantages of Solar Stills:

• They can purify water from nontraditional sources, including soil, plants, and saltwater.

• Solar distillation uses natural energy, meaning you don't need to rely on fire or tools.

Considerations:

• Solar stills work best in sunny, dry climates. In overcast or shaded areas, the rate of condensation will be significantly reduced.

• Constructing multiple stills may be necessary to produce enough water for long-term survival.

IMPROVISED METHODS: USING VEGETATION AND CONDENSATION

Another effective way to gather purified water is through vegetation and condensation methods, particularly in arid or desert environments where traditional water sources may be scarce.

1. Transpiration Bags:

- Use a clear plastic bag to collect water from trees and shrubs. Place the bag over a leafy branch, securing it tightly at the base. The sun's heat will cause the leaves to release moisture, which will collect as condensation inside the bag. This method can yield small amounts of water throughout the day and works well when combined with other techniques.

2. Bamboo Drip Method (Tropical Environments):

- In tropical forests, bamboo can act as a natural water reservoir. Many species of bamboo store water in their nodes. By cutting the bamboo at the right angle, you can collect the water that drips out. It's important to purify this water through boiling or filtering if possible, as it may contain bacteria.

3. Rock Condensation:

- Rocks can be used to collect dew and condensation during cool nights and mornings. Place rocks in a shaded area where condensation is likely to form overnight. In the morning, tilt the rocks to drain the collected moisture into a container. While the amount may be minimal, it can be a vital supplement in desert environments.

FINAL CONSIDERATIONS

Purifying water in the wilderness is a critical skill that requires adaptability and knowledge of various techniques. Combining location skills (like finding natural springs or following animal tracks) with practical methods of filtration and purification ensures you have multiple ways to access and prepare safe drinking water. Practice these skills in different environments to gain confidence and competence, making you more self-sufficient in any survival situation.

BOOK 7
FORAGING FOR EDIBLE PLANTS

Foraging for edible plants is one of the most rewarding and essential skills for long-term wilderness survival. Knowing how to identify, harvest, and prepare edible plants can provide a sustainable and nutritious food source that complements hunting and fishing efforts. However, foraging requires a careful and informed approach. Mistakes in plant identification can lead to severe illness or even death, while unsustainable harvesting practices can deplete resources, disrupting the ecosystem and making long-term survival impossible. This chapter focuses on safely identifying edible plants and harvesting sustainably to ensure that nature continues to provide for you over extended periods.

IDENTIFYING EDIBLE PLANTS SAFELY

The ability to identify edible plants in the wild is a skill that must be developed through practice and study. Many edible plants have toxic look-alikes, and mistaking one for another can be dangerous. The golden rule of foraging is never to consume anything you are not 100% certain about. Knowledge is your first and most important tool; investing time in learning about local flora is crucial before consuming any wild plants.

Start by familiarizing yourself with the most common edible plants in the region you plan to inhabit. In North America, for example, plants like dandelions, wild garlic, clover, plantain, and burdock are widespread and easily recognizable. In other regions, the list may vary, but the principle remains the same: build a foundation of knowledge around common and easily identifiable plants first. This reduces the risk of consuming something harmful while building your confidence as a forager.

When learning to identify plants, pay close attention to multiple features, such as the shape of the leaves, the structure of the stem, the color and size of the flowers, and the smell. Toxic plants may resemble edible ones in one or two aspects but often differ in other areas. For example, the highly toxic water hemlock looks similar to edible members of the carrot family, such as wild carrot (Queen Anne's lace), but it has distinct purple blotches on its stem and a different leaf structure. Observing these subtleties and learning how to recognize them is critical for safe foraging.

THE UNIVERSAL EDIBILITY TEST

If you find yourself in a new area or unsure of a plant's safety, the Universal Edibility Test can be used as a last resort. This method, while time-consuming and not foolproof, can help determine whether a plant is safe to eat. Here's how it works:

1. Separate and Inspect:

* Break the plant into its parts (leaves, stems, roots, and flowers) and inspect them individually. Smell each part to detect any pungent or unusual odors, as many toxic plants have a distinctive smell.

2. Touch Test:

* Rub a small portion of the plant on the inside of your wrist or elbow and wait 15 minutes to see if there is any adverse reaction, such as a rash or itching. If no reaction occurs, proceed to the next step.

3. Taste Test:

* Place a tiny portion of the plant on your tongue and hold it there for 15 minutes. If you experience any tingling, burning, or bitterness, spit it out immediately and rinse your mouth with water. If there's no reaction, chew a small piece without swallowing it, waiting another 15 minutes for any adverse effects.

4. Swallow a Small Amount:

* If no negative effects occur, swallow a small piece and wait several hours to monitor for symptoms like nausea, cramping, or dizziness. If there are no symptoms, the plant may be safe to consume in small quantities.

While the Universal Edibility Test is a useful emergency measure, it should be used with caution and only when absolutely necessary. It's far better to become familiar with a range of safe, edible plants before venturing into the wilderness.

SAFE FORAGING PRACTICES

To forage safely, always carry a reliable field guide for the area you are exploring. These guides often include detailed illustrations and descriptions, making it easier to verify plant characteristics. When foraging, avoid areas that may have been contaminated by pesticides or pollution, such as roadside ditches, industrial zones, or areas near agricultural fields. Plants absorb chemicals from their environment, and consuming those grown in polluted areas can be hazardous.

Another important consideration is the season. Certain plants are only edible at specific stages of their growth cycle. For instance, dandelions are best harvested in the spring when their leaves are tender, while their roots are more nutritious in the fall. Understanding the growth cycle of each plant ensures that you harvest them when they are most nutritious and least likely to be harmful. For example, some plants that are edible when young become toxic as they mature, such as fiddlehead ferns, which must be harvested before they unfurl.

HARVESTING SUSTAINABLY TO PRESERVE NATURE

Foraging should always be conducted with respect for nature and a commitment to sustainability. Taking only what you need and leaving enough for the plants to regenerate ensures that you can continue to rely on them as a resource for the long term. Overharvesting not only depletes a vital food source but also disrupts the ecosystem, affecting the animals and insects that rely on the same plants.

When harvesting, always follow the rule of thirds: take no more than one-third of any plant or plant population in the area. This allows the plants to continue growing and ensures there will be enough for future foraging. For example, when gathering wild garlic or ramps, a popular wild edible, it's crucial to leave enough bulbs in the ground for the plant to regenerate the following season. Uprooting an entire patch can wipe out the plant from that location, which may take years to recover.

Another principle is rotating harvesting locations. Avoid visiting the same spot repeatedly, as this can lead to depletion. Instead, spread your foraging efforts over a wider area, allowing time for plants in one location to recover before harvesting again. This approach mimics the natural grazing patterns of herbivores, who rarely deplete one area entirely before moving on.

HARVESTING ROOTS, LEAVES, AND FRUITS

When foraging for roots, such as burdock, wild carrot, or cattail, it's essential to do so in a way that preserves the plant's ability to grow back. Dig carefully around the root to minimize damage to surrounding plants and avoid uprooting the entire plant unless necessary. In many cases, cutting part of the root and leaving the rest intact allows the plant to continue growing, ensuring it remains a viable food source in the future.

For leafy greens like dandelion, plantain, and nettles, harvesting sustainably involves taking only a few leaves from each plant rather than stripping it entirely. This allows the plant to continue photosynthesizing and growing. Picking leaves during the morning, when they are still fresh and moist, also ensures they retain their nutrients.

Fruits and berries, such as wild raspberries, blackberries, or blueberries, are generally safe to harvest in larger quantities, as taking the fruit does not harm the plant itself. However, it's important to leave some fruit behind, as many animals rely on these berries for food, and the plant uses them to reproduce. By being mindful of your impact, you help maintain the balance between human needs and the ecosystem.

FORAGING FOR NUTS, SEEDS, AND MUSHROOMS

In late summer and fall, nuts and seeds become available and are excellent sources of protein and fat. Acorns, hazelnuts, and walnuts are common examples, but they often require processing to be edible. Acorns, for example, contain tannins that must be leached out through soaking and boiling before they become safe to eat. While collecting nuts, it's crucial to leave a portion behind for wildlife and to ensure that the trees can continue to propagate.

When it comes to mushrooms, foraging requires an even greater level of expertise. Many mushrooms have toxic look-alikes that can be deadly. It's important to become familiar with a few easily recognizable edible varieties, such as chanterelles, morels, or puffballs, and learn their unique characteristics. For example, chanterelles have a distinct funnel shape and an apricot-like aroma, while puffballs are unmistakable when they are young and completely white inside.

Always check for identification marks specific to each mushroom type, as the consequences of misidentification can be severe. Avoid picking mushrooms that are damaged, old, or growing near pollution sources, as they may absorb harmful substances. When harvesting mushrooms, cut them at the base rather than pulling them up, to protect the mycelium network in the soil, which allows more mushrooms to grow in the future.

PREPARING AND COOKING WILD EDIBLES

Even when a plant is identified as safe and harvested sustainably, proper preparation is essential to ensure it is nutritious and palatable. Some plants, like nettles, are best cooked to neutralize irritating compounds, while others, like dock leaves, may require boiling to remove bitterness. Learning how to cook and process wild foods is just as important as identifying them.

Cooking methods such as boiling, roasting, or drying can improve flavor and texture while also enhancing the nutritional value. For instance, the roots of burdock and dandelion can be boiled or roasted, transforming their texture and making them more digestible. By experimenting with different preparation methods, you can make the most of the resources you harvest and create a varied and sustainable diet in the wilderness.

BUILDING YOUR KNOWLEDGE BASE

Foraging is a skill that grows over time. Start by learning a few easy-to-identify plants and gradually expand your repertoire. Take notes on where and when certain plants grow, as this will help build a mental map of your environment's resources. Studying edible plants during different seasons also helps, as many plants look different when they flower versus when they are in their vegetative stage.

By gaining experience and gradually broadening your knowledge, you become more confident in identifying and preparing wild edibles, making it easier to rely on foraging as a sustainable food source.

CONCLUSION

Foraging for edible plants is a vital skill for anyone interested in long-term wilderness survival. By learning to identify plants safely, practicing sustainable harvesting methods, and understanding how to prepare wild edibles, you not only nourish yourself but also protect the delicate balance of the ecosystem. This practice of respect and sustainability ensures that the wilderness remains a reliable source of food, providing for both present and future needs. Developing this skill set turns the wilderness into a bountiful environment, enriching the survival experience while enhancing your connection with nature.

BOOK 8
HUNTING AND TRAPPING BASICS

Hunting and trapping are crucial skills for long-term wilderness survival, especially when other food sources like plants or nuts are scarce. While foraging provides essential nutrients, hunting offers protein and fats that are vital for energy and sustenance, particularly during cold weather or physically demanding activities. This chapter focuses on the foundational aspects of hunting and trapping, including building snares and improvised traps, ethical and sustainable hunting practices, and fishing without modern gear. By mastering these skills, you can enhance your ability to secure food consistently while maintaining balance and respect for the natural environment.

BUILDING SNARES AND IMPROVISED TRAPS

In a survival situation, snares and traps are invaluable tools for catching small game. They allow you to conserve energy by passively hunting; once set, snares work on their own, increasing your chances of catching food while you attend to other tasks like building shelter, purifying water, or gathering firewood. Building effective snares requires an understanding of animal behavior, as well as the ability to use available materials creatively.

The Basics of Snares and Traps

Snares are designed to capture animals such as rabbits, squirrels, and other small mammals by trapping them in a loop of cordage. The loop tightens when the animal passes through it, holding the prey until it can be retrieved. A well-constructed snare can be made from a variety of materials, including paracord, wire, or even improvised natural fibers like vines or strips of bark.

The most important aspect of building a snare is placement. Snares must be positioned on animal trails or near burrows and food sources, where animals are likely to pass through. To identify these trails, look for signs like tracks, droppings, or trampled vegetation. Rabbits, for instance, tend to use the same trails repeatedly, making it easier to predict their movements.

Simple Snare:

- Find a branch or sapling that is flexible but strong. It should be able to bend without breaking and should return to its original position when released.
- Cut a length of cordage or wire, forming a loop that is slightly larger than the animal you are targeting. Attach one end of the cord to the sapling and position the loop at head height

for the animal. Ensure the snare is loose enough to close quickly when the animal moves through it.

- Secure the sapling to the ground with a stake or other anchor to prevent the animal from dragging the entire snare away.

The tension of the sapling pulls the loop tight when the animal moves through, effectively trapping it. This is known as a spring snare and is particularly effective for small, fast-moving animals.

Deadfall Trap:

- Another effective trap is the deadfall, which uses a heavy object, like a log or rock, balanced on a support stick that is connected to a trigger. When the animal disturbs the baited trigger, the heavy object falls, trapping or killing the animal instantly.
- Deadfall traps require careful balancing of the support stick and trigger. Bait, such as nuts or small pieces of fruit, is placed strategically to encourage the animal to disturb the trap.

Deadfall traps are effective because they don't rely on cordage and can be set up using only natural materials. However, they must be constructed carefully to avoid false triggers or injuries while setting them up.

ETHICAL AND SUSTAINABLE HUNTING PRACTICES

While hunting and trapping are necessary for survival, it is crucial to approach these activities with a sense of ethics and responsibility. Overhunting or indiscriminate trapping can disrupt local ecosystems, deplete wildlife populations, and make long-term survival unsustainable. Practicing ethical and sustainable hunting ensures that you can continue to rely on the environment for food without causing harm to the balance of nature.

Understanding Seasonal Cycles

Animals have seasonal cycles that dictate when they are most active, mating, or raising young. Understanding these cycles is essential for ethical hunting. For instance, hunting animals during their breeding season can have severe impacts on populations, as removing one animal might leave young without a caregiver, leading to their deaths. It's important to observe animal behavior and recognize signs of breeding or nesting before setting traps.

In survival situations, targeting animals that are not currently breeding and avoiding those that may have dependent young increases the likelihood that wildlife populations will remain stable. By doing so, you ensure that the ecosystem can regenerate, providing a sustainable food source over time.

The Rule of Selective Hunting

Selective hunting is about choosing the right prey based on your needs and the availability of game. It's better to target smaller animals, like rabbits or squirrels, that reproduce quickly and have less impact on the overall ecosystem. Larger game, such as deer, should only be hunted if absolutely necessary, as taking down a large animal has a much greater impact on the local environment. Additionally, processing and storing large amounts of meat in the wilderness can be challenging, especially in warm climates where preserving meat is difficult.

When hunting larger animals, use every part of the animal to minimize waste. The meat can be smoked or dried for long-term storage, bones can be fashioned into tools, and fur can be used for insulation or clothing. Utilizing every part of the animal not only honors the life taken but also maximizes the benefits of the hunt, ensuring nothing is wasted.

Rotating Hunting Areas

To maintain wildlife populations, it's important to rotate hunting and trapping areas. Constantly hunting in the same location can quickly deplete resources, making it harder to find food in the future. By rotating areas, you give time for animals to repopulate and allow habitats to recover. This strategy mimics the natural behavior of predators, who tend to migrate through their territories, allowing prey populations to regenerate.

Additionally, avoiding areas where animals gather to breed or rear young helps maintain healthy populations. Observing animal trails and understanding their patterns over time allows you to identify the best spots for trapping without disrupting breeding grounds.

FISHING WITHOUT MODERN GEAR

Fishing is a highly effective and energy-efficient way to secure food in the wilderness, especially if you are near rivers, lakes, or coastal areas. Fish provide a valuable source of protein and fats that are essential for maintaining energy levels and health. However, catching fish without modern rods, reels, or nets requires creativity and resourcefulness.

Primitive Fishing Techniques

Spearfishing:

- Spearfishing is one of the oldest and simplest methods of fishing. To create a spear, find a straight, sturdy stick and sharpen the tip. For improved accuracy and effectiveness, split the tip into prongs, creating a barbed spear that can hold fish more securely when they are struck.
- Spearfishing works best in shallow, clear waters where fish can be seen easily. Slowly approach the water, staying as still as possible to avoid startling the fish. When you spot a target, aim below the fish, as water refraction can make fish appear higher than they actually are. Spearfishing requires patience and practice, but once mastered, it can be a reliable way to catch fish.

Fish Traps:

- Fish traps, like weirs or baskets, allow for passive fishing. A weir is a barrier constructed across a stream or river that guides fish into a confined area or trap. It is typically built using rocks, logs, or sticks arranged in a V-shape with the open end facing upstream. As fish swim downstream, they are funneled into the narrow end, where they become trapped.

- Basket traps can be constructed using natural materials such as reeds, vines, or willow branches. By weaving these materials into a cylindrical shape with an entrance that tapers inward, fish can swim into the basket but find it difficult to escape. Bait can be placed inside the trap to attract fish. This method is particularly effective in shallow waters or along the banks of lakes.

Hand Fishing (Noodling):

- In shallow streams or rivers, noodling is a technique where fish are caught by hand. This method works well for catching species like catfish, which tend to hide under rocks or in submerged logs. To noodle, carefully feel under rocks or into holes where fish might hide, and grab the fish when you locate one. While this technique is straightforward, it can be risky if you're unaware of other animals like snakes or snapping turtles, which may also inhabit these spaces.

IMPROVISED FISHING LINES AND HOOKS

Without a fishing rod, improvised fishing lines can be made from various materials, including vines, strips of cloth, or paracord. Hooks can be fashioned from bones, thorns, or even pieces of metal if available. The goal is to create a sturdy enough line and hook system that can hold the weight of the fish without breaking.

Improvised Hooks:

- Bone hooks can be made by sharpening small bones from animals you've hunted. Carve a barb into one end of the bone to secure the fish once it bites.
- If bones are not available, other materials like thorns from bushes or bent pieces of wire can be used. The important thing is to create a sharp point that can pierce and hold.

Bait and Lures:

- Bait for fishing can be found easily in most environments. Earthworms, grubs, or insects are common choices that attract a variety of fish species. In some cases, using small pieces of meat or offal from other animals you've hunted can be effective as well.
- For lures, shiny objects such as shells, stones, or improvised metallic items can be used to catch the attention of fish. By dangling the lure in the water and moving it slowly, you can mimic the movement of prey, enticing fish to strike.

PROCESSING AND PRESERVING GAME AND FISH

After successfully hunting or catching fish, it's vital to process and preserve the food to avoid spoilage, especially in warm climates where bacteria thrive. Knowing how to properly clean and prepare game and fish is essential for maximizing the yield and ensuring the food is safe to eat.

Cleaning and Preparing Small Game:

- Small animals like rabbits, squirrels, or birds should be skinned and gutted as soon as possible. Remove the internal organs, and inspect them for signs of disease. Once cleaned, the meat can be roasted over a fire, boiled in a makeshift pot, or dried for preservation.

- To dry meat, thin strips can be hung near a fire or in the sun, using smoke or heat to remove moisture. This process, known as jerky-making, is ideal for creating lightweight, long-lasting food supplies.

Preserving Fish:

- Fish should be gutted immediately, and the scales removed if necessary. To preserve fish for long-term use, smoking is one of the most effective methods. Create a small, enclosed frame with branches and cover it with leaves or bark to hold in the smoke. Hang the fish inside and let it smoke slowly, preserving it for days or weeks.

- Alternatively, drying fish in the sun can also work in hot, dry climates. Place fish on a clean surface exposed to the sun, turning them regularly to ensure even drying.

CONCLUSION

Hunting, trapping, and fishing without modern tools are essential skills for any wilderness survivalist. These techniques require patience, practice, and an ethical approach to maintain balance with nature. By mastering snares, understanding animal behavior, practicing sustainable hunting practices, and improvising effective fishing methods, you ensure that you have access to essential protein and fat, which are crucial for long-term survival. Ultimately, these skills not only enhance your chances of surviving but also deepen your connection to the natural world, teaching you to live in harmony with the environment while meeting your needs responsibly.

BOOK 9
NATURAL MEDICINE

The wilderness offers an abundant pharmacy of plants and herbs that can be used for treating a wide range of ailments, from cuts and wounds to digestive issues and respiratory problems. Understanding how to identify, prepare, and safely administer these natural medicines is a vital skill for anyone living off the land. While modern medicine may not always be available in a survival situation, nature provides alternatives that, when used correctly, can be highly effective. This chapter explores the fundamentals of natural medicine, focusing on identifying medicinal plants, preparing herbal remedies for common ailments, and administering these treatments safely in a wilderness environment.

IDENTIFYING MEDICINAL PLANTS

Identifying medicinal plants is the first and most crucial step in utilizing natural medicine effectively. The wilderness is filled with plants that offer medicinal properties, but it also harbors many that are toxic and potentially dangerous if misidentified. Therefore, it is essential to develop a keen understanding of local flora and to be able to distinguish beneficial plants from harmful ones with confidence.

One of the most important principles of identifying medicinal plants is to rely on multiple characteristics rather than just one or two. For example, observing the shape of the leaves, the texture of the stem, the color and structure of the flowers, and even the scent of the plant can provide essential clues. While one feature may be shared by many species, a combination of characteristics is often unique to a specific plant. For instance, yarrow, a common medicinal herb, has distinct feathery leaves, white clusters of small flowers, and a slightly bitter, aromatic scent. By learning to recognize these details, you can reliably identify it and use it for its well-known properties, such as stopping bleeding and reducing inflammation.

It is also crucial to study plants throughout their life cycles, as they can look dramatically different depending on the season. A plant that is safe and medicinal in the spring may develop toxic properties as it matures in the summer. Others may lose their medicinal value as they flower or bear fruit. For example, the leaves of plantain, a versatile medicinal plant, are most potent when harvested young. As the plant grows and its leaves become larger and tougher, their healing properties diminish. Knowing when to harvest plants is as important as knowing where to find them.

Traditional knowledge and field guides are invaluable resources for learning about medicinal plants. Field guides often provide detailed illustrations and descriptions, helping you identify plants with greater accuracy. Additionally, traditional wisdom—passed down through generations—offers insights into the uses of specific plants that might not be covered in written guides. Indigenous communities and seasoned herbalists, for instance, often have extensive knowledge of local flora, making them valuable sources of information when learning to identify medicinal plants safely.

PREPARING HERBAL REMEDIES FOR COMMON AILMENTS

Once you have identified medicinal plants, the next step is learning how to prepare them effectively. Preparation methods vary depending on the ailment being treated and the plant's properties. Some plants are best used fresh, while others must be dried or boiled to release their active compounds. The three most common forms of preparation in the wild are teas, poultices, and tinctures.

Teas are perhaps the simplest and most versatile method of extracting medicinal properties from plants. By boiling or steeping leaves, flowers, or roots in water, you can create a drinkable infusion that delivers the plant's benefits. For example, brewing the flowers of chamomile can help soothe anxiety and promote sleep, while a tea made from peppermint leaves can alleviate digestive issues. Teas are effective for treating internal ailments like colds, indigestion, and mild fevers, as they allow the body to absorb the healing properties directly through the digestive system.

Poultices are another effective method, especially for external injuries such as cuts, bruises, or insect bites. To make a poultice, mash fresh leaves, flowers, or roots into a paste, which is then applied directly to the affected area. Yarrow, for example, is a powerful plant that, when crushed and applied as a poultice, can help stop bleeding and disinfect wounds. Plantain leaves are another excellent choice, as they can draw out toxins and reduce inflammation when applied to insect stings or rashes. Poultices work best with fresh plant material, which means they need to be prepared and applied immediately after harvesting.

Tinctures, on the other hand, are a more concentrated form of herbal medicine that can be used for long-term storage. Tinctures are made by soaking medicinal plants in alcohol, which extracts and preserves the active compounds. The resulting solution can be used in small doses to treat a variety of conditions. For instance, a tincture made from echinacea roots can be used to boost the immune system, while one made from valerian root may help with insomnia. While tinctures require a bit more preparation and access to alcohol, they are a valuable way to create a long-lasting supply of medicine.

Drying and storing herbs is another crucial aspect of preparation, especially for long-term survival situations. Drying herbs preserves them for later use, allowing you to create teas or poultices when fresh plants are not available. The best way to dry herbs in the wild is to place them in a shaded, well-ventilated area, hanging them upside down if possible to allow air to circulate. Once dried, the herbs can be crushed into a powder or stored as whole leaves in a dry container. Properly dried and stored herbs can remain effective for months, providing a reliable source of medicine when needed.

SAFELY ADMINISTERING NATURAL TREATMENTS

While natural remedies can be highly effective, it is important to administer them safely to avoid adverse effects. Unlike pharmaceutical medications, which are standardized and dosage-controlled, herbal medicine requires careful consideration of dosage and preparation to ensure safety and efficacy. Some plants can be harmful if consumed in large quantities or if taken without proper knowledge of their effects.

One of the first steps in administering natural treatments safely is to start with small doses and observe the body's response. If you are using a new herb or plant for the first time, begin with a minimal amount, such as a few drops of a tincture or a small sip of tea, and wait to see if any adverse reactions occur. Symptoms like nausea, dizziness, or skin irritation can indicate an allergic reaction or sensitivity, and further use should be avoided.

It's also important to understand which parts of the plant are safe to use. In some cases, only the leaves or flowers may be edible, while other parts of the plant may be toxic. For example, elderberry is a widely used medicinal plant known for its immune-boosting properties, but its leaves, stems, and unripe berries contain cyanogenic glycosides, which can be toxic if ingested. Proper knowledge of plant anatomy is essential to prevent poisoning and ensure that only the safe and beneficial parts are used.

Timing and dosage are critical factors in herbal medicine. Some herbs, such as mint or ginger, can be used frequently and in large amounts without issue. Others, like willow bark (a natural source of salicylic acid, the precursor to aspirin), must be used with caution, as excessive consumption can cause stomach irritation or other side effects. Understanding the potency of each plant and adjusting the dosage accordingly is essential for safely managing ailments without overuse.

Additionally, certain conditions or ailments require specific methods of treatment. For example, an upset stomach may be treated with a mild tea made from peppermint or ginger, while a more serious wound may need a poultice made from antiseptic plants like yarrow or calendula. In some cases, multiple treatments may need to be combined. For instance, a deep wound might benefit from a yarrow poultice to stop bleeding, followed by a tea made from antimicrobial herbs like sage to fight infection from within. Knowing how to combine different remedies for a holistic approach enhances the effectiveness of natural medicine.

Another critical consideration when administering herbal remedies is knowing when professional medical help is necessary. Natural medicine can be effective for many ailments, but it may not be sufficient for serious conditions such as deep infections, broken bones, or poisoning. In such cases, recognizing the limits of herbal treatment and seeking medical help as soon as possible is essential. In a survival scenario, this may involve knowing how to stabilize the patient and manage symptoms until professional care becomes available.

Lastly, maintaining a detailed record of herbal treatments is a good practice. Keeping notes on which herbs were used, in what quantities, and for what purposes allows you to track their effectiveness and note any side effects or reactions. This practice not only improves your understanding of natural medicine but also ensures that you can refine and adjust treatments as needed.

CONCLUSION

Mastering the use of natural medicine is an invaluable skill for wilderness survival. By learning to identify medicinal plants accurately, preparing effective remedies, and administering treatments safely, you can manage a range of common ailments and injuries without relying on modern pharmaceuticals. However, this skill requires a deep respect for nature and a commitment to ongoing learning. Plants can be powerful allies, but they must be approached with caution and knowledge to be used safely and effectively. Developing this expertise not only enhances your self-sufficiency but also deepens your connection to the natural world, allowing you to harness its resources responsibly and sustainably.

BOOK 10
NAVIGATION WITHOUT TECHNOLOGY

In a world increasingly dependent on technology for navigation, the ability to find your way in the wilderness without the aid of GPS devices or digital maps is an invaluable skill. Navigating through the wilderness using only natural cues requires a deep understanding of the environment and the ability to read the subtle signs that nature provides. Whether it's relying on the sun and stars, interpreting landmarks, or constructing improvised compasses, these techniques allow you to orient yourself accurately and travel with confidence. This chapter will delve into these essential methods, helping you navigate even the most unfamiliar terrain with a sense of certainty and control.

USING THE SUN AND STARS FOR ORIENTATION

One of the most fundamental skills in wilderness navigation is the ability to use the sun and stars to determine direction. These celestial bodies are reliable constants, providing consistent points of reference that help orient you in the absence of technology. While the sun and stars offer effective guidance, understanding how to interpret their movements accurately is crucial.

Using the Sun for Daytime Navigation

During the day, the sun can be a powerful tool for establishing your bearings. The sun rises in the east and sets in the west, providing two fixed points that can help determine cardinal directions. At midday, when the sun is at its highest point in the sky, it is generally due south in the northern hemisphere and north in the southern hemisphere. This principle forms the foundation of solar navigation.

To determine direction more precisely, you can use the shadow stick method. This method involves placing a stick vertically in the ground on a sunny day and marking the tip of the shadow it casts. After about 15 minutes, you'll notice that the shadow has moved. Mark the new position of the shadow's tip and draw a straight line between the two points—this line runs roughly east to west, with the first mark indicating west and the second mark pointing east. By standing with the east point on your right and the west point on your left, you can now identify north directly ahead of you and south behind.

The sun's position also changes seasonally. In the northern hemisphere during summer, the sun rises northeast and sets northwest, while in winter, it rises southeast and sets southwest. This shift affects the length and angle of shadows, so it's important to understand these variations and adjust your interpretation accordingly.

Using the Stars for Nighttime Navigation

When the sun sets, the stars become your primary tool for orientation. The night sky is filled with constellations that have been used for millennia by explorers and travelers to find their way. In the northern hemisphere, the North Star, or Polaris, is an invaluable reference point. Polaris is located directly above the North Pole, meaning it always indicates true north. To find Polaris, locate the Big Dipper constellation (Ursa Major). The two stars at the end of the Big Dipper's "bowl" form a line that points directly to Polaris. Once you've found Polaris, you know the direction of true north, which allows you to orient yourself and determine the other cardinal points.

In the southern hemisphere, there is no equivalent to Polaris, but the Southern Cross constellation can serve a similar purpose. The Southern Cross is a small but prominent constellation, and its longer axis points towards the south celestial pole. By extending this axis about four and a half times its length, you can find a point in the sky that indicates true south. Additionally, the Two Pointers—two bright stars that appear near the Southern Cross—can help confirm its location.

Learning to read the night sky requires practice and familiarity with these constellations. It's helpful to spend time observing the stars in different locations and conditions, as cloud cover, moonlight, or light pollution can obscure some stars. Once you become comfortable locating these key constellations, navigating by the stars can become an intuitive and reliable skill.

READING NATURAL LANDMARKS FOR GUIDANCE

Natural landmarks provide another layer of navigational support, helping you maintain orientation when celestial bodies are not visible due to weather conditions or dense canopy cover. Knowing how to read and interpret these landmarks—such as rivers, mountain ranges, and vegetation patterns—can guide you through complex terrains.

Interpreting Rivers and Streams

Waterways are often reliable guides, as they flow downhill and typically merge into larger bodies of water like lakes, rivers, or the sea. By following the flow of a stream or river, you can often navigate your way to lower elevations or more populated areas. However, it's crucial to recognize that rivers may not always take a direct path; they meander, split, or form oxbow lakes, so using them for navigation requires flexibility and awareness of the terrain. When crossing rivers, always ensure it is safe to do so, as swift currents can be dangerous.

Mountain Ranges and Ridge Lines

Mountains and ridge lines are prominent natural features that can serve as orientation tools, especially in expansive wilderness areas. Ridge lines generally run along the high points of mountain ranges and can guide you in a specific direction. For instance, if you know the general orientation of a mountain range (e.g., running north to south), following a ridge line can help keep you on course.

Mountains often cast shadows that indicate direction. In the early morning, the eastern side of a mountain is lit by the rising sun, while in the evening, the western side is illuminated. Observing these shadow patterns, along with the knowledge of the sun's behavior, can help you determine your orientation even in areas with limited visibility.

Vegetation and Tree Growth

Vegetation patterns also provide clues about direction and elevation. In the northern hemisphere, for example, the south-facing slopes of hills and mountains typically receive more sunlight and, therefore, have different vegetation than the north-facing slopes. South-facing slopes may have more lush, sun-loving plants, while the north-facing slopes often support moss and shade-tolerant species. Trees themselves can also indicate direction. For instance, moss tends to grow on the north side of trees in northern temperate zones, where sunlight is less direct. While this method is not foolproof (as environmental factors can influence moss growth), it can be a helpful supplementary guide when combined with other cues.

Wind and Weather Patterns

Wind direction and weather patterns can also aid navigation. In many regions, prevailing winds blow from specific directions. For example, in parts of the United States, the westerlies (winds blowing from west to east) are common. Observing the direction from which wind consistently blows can give you a general sense of direction. Similarly, cloud movement and patterns, such as the approach of storm systems, often follow predictable paths that can indicate where certain landmarks or terrain features might be located.

CREATING IMPROVISED COMPASSES

When the sun, stars, or landmarks are unavailable or unclear, creating an improvised compass can provide a quick and effective means of determining direction. A simple, improvised compass can be constructed using basic materials found in most environments, such as a needle, a magnet (or a substitute), and water.

Magnetizing a Needle

The first step in making an improvised compass is to magnetize a small metal object, such as a needle or a straightened paper clip. If you have access to a magnet, simply rub the needle along the magnet repeatedly in the same direction. This action aligns the atoms in the needle, turning it into a temporary magnet capable of aligning with the Earth's magnetic field. If you don't have a magnet, you can also magnetize the needle by rubbing it with silk or wool, or by stroking it along your hair. Although less effective, these methods can still induce enough magnetism to work as a basic compass.

Floating the Needle

Once magnetized, the needle needs to be floated so it can pivot freely and align with magnetic north. Find a small container of water, such as a leaf, a piece of bark, or even a water-filled cap, and float a piece of lightweight material (a leaf or small piece of wood) on the surface. Carefully place the needle on top of the material, ensuring that it floats freely without obstruction. The needle should slowly rotate and align itself with magnetic north and south. It's important to let it settle for a moment to ensure that it has correctly oriented itself.

Interpreting the Compass

Once the needle has settled, the direction it points indicates magnetic north. In most cases, magnetic north is slightly off from true north due to the Earth's magnetic declination. The difference between true and magnetic north varies depending on your location. For example, in the western United States, magnetic north may deviate to the east, while in the eastern part of the country, it may veer to the west. If you are familiar with the declination in your area, you can adjust your navigation accordingly. Without this information, however, using magnetic north as a general guide will still provide a reliable sense of direction.

Shadow Compass Technique

Another method of creating an improvised compass is the shadow compass. This technique is particularly useful on clear days when the sun is visible. To make a shadow compass, place a stick upright in the ground and mark the tip of its shadow. Wait about 15-30 minutes, then mark the new position of the shadow's tip. Draw a straight line between the two points—this line indicates an east-to-west orientation. By standing with your left foot on the first mark (west) and your right foot on the second mark (east), you can determine that true north is directly ahead.

This method is particularly effective because it does not require any additional tools beyond a stick and sunlight, making it accessible in most conditions. However, it is dependent on clear skies, and its accuracy can be influenced by the time of day. The shadow method works best around midday when the sun is high and shadows are shorter.

NAVIGATING WITHOUT TECHNOLOGY: PRACTICE AND PRECISION

The methods outlined above are not foolproof; they require practice and experience to use effectively. Navigating without technology is a skill that involves constant observation, adaptation, and a willingness to learn from the environment. Even seasoned explorers make use of multiple techniques simultaneously to verify their direction and ensure accuracy.

The more familiar you become with these methods, the more intuitive they will become. Practice using the sun, stars, and landmarks in familiar areas before relying on them in unknown territories. Test the effectiveness of your improvised compass techniques in different environments and under varying conditions. Observe the changes in plant growth and animal behavior across different regions to enhance your understanding of how natural features correlate with direction.

By honing these skills, you transform your relationship with the wilderness. Instead of relying on technology, you learn to read the landscape and sky as reliable guides. This ability not only increases your chances of survival but also deepens your connection with the natural world, enabling you to navigate confidently and sustainably wherever you may find yourself.

BOOK 11
CREATING AND USING MAPS

In wilderness survival, having a map is a powerful asset. However, in the absence of professionally made maps or digital tools, the ability to create and use maps using natural landmarks, mental strategies, and basic tools becomes invaluable. Maps, whether they are physical drawings or mental guides, provide orientation, help track your location, and offer a sense of control when navigating unknown terrain. This chapter covers drawing mental maps for orientation, using simple tools for physical mapping, and navigating unfamiliar areas safely. By developing these skills, you can enhance your ability to move confidently and efficiently through the wilderness.

DRAWING MENTAL MAPS FOR ORIENTATION

A mental map is an internal representation of an area that you build using your observations, memory, and knowledge of the terrain. It doesn't involve physical drawings or tools but rather relies on your ability to note and recall significant features of the environment, such as rivers, mountains, trails, and other landmarks. Mental mapping is particularly useful when you lack paper or mapping tools and must rely solely on your perception and memory to navigate.

To create a mental map, you need to engage all your senses and be observant of your surroundings. It begins with breaking down the area into key features that are easy to recognize and recall. For example, you might note a distinctive mountain peak to the north, a river cutting through the valley, and a large oak tree that stands out from the rest of the forest. These elements serve as anchor points in your mental map, helping you establish directions and distances as you move.

Techniques for Drawing Mental Maps

1. Using the Cardinal Directions:

*   The first step in developing an accurate mental map is to establish the four cardinal directions: north, south, east, and west. You can do this using the sun, stars, or natural landmarks. Once you know where these directions are, orient yourself and keep track of your movement relative to them.

2. Identifying Key Landmarks:

*   Observe your surroundings for distinctive natural features such as ridges, streams, cliffs, or lakes. These landmarks are easier to remember and can be used as reference points. For instance, if you know that a river runs north to south through the area, you can use it to reorient yourself if you get lost.

3. Tracking Distances and Time:

- Estimating distances is an important part of mental mapping. You can gauge distances based on the time it takes to walk between landmarks. For instance, if it takes an hour to walk from a mountain base to a lake, you now have a rough idea of how far apart these two points are.

- Use pacing techniques (e.g., counting steps) to keep track of distances. For example, 1000 steps might equal approximately half a mile, depending on your stride.

4. Visualizing the Landscape:

- Create a mental image of the landscape based on the landmarks you've identified. Visualize where these features are in relation to one another. Imagine yourself moving through the terrain, keeping these key points in your mind as a guide.

- Adjust and update your mental map as you move and encounter new features. This ensures that your internal map remains accurate and reflective of the actual terrain.

Tips for Effective Mental Mapping

TIP	EXPLANATION
Use landmarks consistently	Rely on prominent features like mountains, rivers, or unique trees to maintain consistency in orientation.
Practice observation skills	Improve your ability to note subtle changes in the environment that may be helpful for navigation.
Update your map frequently	Adapt your mental map with new information as you explore, ensuring it remains accurate.
Remember cardinal directions	Regularly check the sun's position or other indicators to maintain your sense of direction.

USING SIMPLE TOOLS FOR PHYSICAL MAPPING

While mental maps are effective for short-term navigation, creating physical maps using simple tools is invaluable for tracking and planning longer journeys. Physical maps give you a visual representation of your surroundings and allow for more detailed plotting of routes, distances, and features. Even if you don't have professional equipment, you can create effective maps using rudimentary tools and materials found in the wilderness.

Basic Tools for Physical Mapping

- Sticks and Stones: These can be used to draw outlines of terrain features on flat surfaces such as dirt or sand. This method is temporary but effective when you need to discuss routes or explain terrain features to others in your group.

- **Charcoal or Burnt Wood:** Charcoal from a campfire can be used as a pencil to draw maps on tree bark, large leaves, or rocks.
- **Cordage or String:** Use string to measure distances between points, which can then be translated into approximate distances on a map.
- **Paper-like Materials:** If you have access to paper, bark, or even fabric, these can serve as canvases for drawing more permanent maps.

Steps to Create a Simple Physical Map

1. Select a Flat Surface:

- If you are drawing a temporary map, find a patch of flat ground where you can use sticks and stones to create a map outline. For more permanent maps, use bark, fabric, or any material that can hold charcoal markings.

2. Mark the Cardinal Directions:

- Begin by marking the four cardinal directions at the edges of your map. This will help keep your drawing oriented correctly and consistent with the landscape.

3. Add Major Landmarks:

- Start by sketching the most prominent features first, such as mountain ranges, rivers, or lakes. These will act as anchor points on your map. Make sure their relative positions are accurate to the best of your ability.

4. Fill in Secondary Details:

- Add smaller features, such as trails, clearings, rock formations, or campsites, as you discover them. Use symbols or labels to distinguish between different types of terrain, like forests, marshes, or plains.

5. Include Scale and Distance Indicators:

- If possible, establish a rough scale based on your own pace or time traveled. For instance, if you walked for an hour between two landmarks, estimate the distance based on your average speed and add it to the map.

By creating a physical map, you not only document your surroundings but also provide a reference for future journeys. It allows you to compare your actual movement with the planned route, helping to refine and improve your navigation over time.

SYMBOL	DESCRIPTION
⊙	Sun direction (East/West)
▽	Mountain peak

≈	River or stream
●	Campsite location
//	Dense forest or wooded area

This basic symbol key helps simplify the map and make it easier to read, even when resources for mapping are limited.

NAVIGATING UNKNOWN TERRAIN SAFELY

Navigating unknown terrain is challenging, especially when you don't have established trails or familiar landmarks to rely on. The key to doing this safely is preparation, caution, and a systematic approach to exploration. By combining mental and physical mapping with careful observation, you can reduce the risks associated with traversing unfamiliar areas and find your way efficiently.

Preparing for the Journey

Before setting out into unknown terrain, gather as much information as possible about the environment. Study the local ecosystem if you have the opportunity; different types of flora and fauna often indicate specific terrain features or water sources. For instance, areas with lush vegetation may indicate nearby water, while barren or rocky landscapes could suggest high elevation or dry conditions.

Having basic survival equipment is also important when navigating unknown terrain. At minimum, carry a reliable knife, materials for fire-starting, and an improvised shelter setup. These essentials help ensure your safety if you need to camp overnight or face unexpected obstacles like adverse weather.

USING TERRAIN AND NATURAL CUES FOR GUIDANCE

As you begin to navigate, use the terrain's natural features to guide your movement. Rivers and streams are particularly useful for orientation because they flow downhill and often lead to larger bodies of water or settlements. Following a river can provide a reliable way to travel through unknown terrain, and if you must move away from the water temporarily, you can use landmarks along the riverbank to find your way back.

When traveling through dense forests or mountainous regions, elevation changes become significant guides. Moving along a ridgeline or staying at higher elevations can provide better visibility, allowing you to spot landmarks in the distance. However, it's important to balance this with the need for shelter and water. Staying too high for too long may expose you to the elements, while lower elevations might offer more shelter and resources.

CREATING REFERENCE POINTS ALONG THE WAY

As you move through unknown terrain, create temporary reference points that you can use to track your progress and retrace your steps if needed. For example, you can pile stones, mark trees with a knife, or lay out small branches in distinctive patterns. These markers act as visual cues that help you confirm your location and direction as you move forward.

Another method is to use natural features as waypoints. A unique rock formation, a distinctive tree, or a hill can serve as a checkpoint. By keeping track of these features, you establish a series of known points that you can reference when navigating. When you encounter new terrain, identify the most prominent feature and use it as your next target, creating a visual "breadcrumb trail" that leads you through the landscape.

SAFE EXPLORATION TECHNIQUES

When venturing into completely uncharted areas, it's important to proceed with caution. Systematic exploration ensures you don't become disoriented or lost. One effective technique is the circular or grid exploration pattern.

To use a circular pattern, start from a known point, such as a campsite or a distinct landmark, and move outward in a circular path, gradually expanding the radius. This allows you to explore the surrounding area while remaining within sight of your starting point. By gradually expanding the circle, you can map out the terrain without losing your way.

Alternatively, you can use a grid pattern. Divide the area into sections mentally or physically by using landmarks. Explore each section thoroughly before moving to the next, ensuring that you cover the terrain methodically and do not stray too far from your starting point.

In both methods, periodically return to your starting point to verify your location and update your maps, whether mental or physical. This approach minimizes the risk of becoming lost and allows you to build a detailed understanding of the area over time.

MANAGING RISKS WHILE NAVIGATING

Navigating unknown terrain carries inherent risks, such as injury, getting lost, or encountering dangerous wildlife. To minimize these risks, move cautiously, avoid traveling alone if possible, and always keep an eye on your surroundings. Avoid venturing too far without marking your path, and ensure that you have enough daylight left to return safely to your base if needed.

COMBINING TECHNIQUES FOR EFFECTIVE NAVIGATION

The most effective navigation in the wilderness often combines multiple techniques. Use the sun, stars, and natural landmarks alongside mental and physical maps to create a comprehensive understanding of the terrain. When these elements work together, they enhance your ability to travel efficiently and safely, even in challenging environments.

CONCLUSION

Mastering the creation and use of maps—whether mental or physical—enables you to navigate through wilderness terrain with confidence. By learning how to interpret natural landmarks, track distances, and combine various mapping techniques, you develop a crucial survival skill that extends beyond technology. Navigating unknown terrain safely requires preparation, careful observation, and the ability to adapt strategies as you encounter new challenges. Practicing these skills builds self-reliance, ensuring that you can confidently explore and survive in any environment.

BOOK 12

WILDERNESS COOKING TECHNIQUES

Cooking in the wilderness is not just about survival; it's about transforming the raw ingredients nature offers into nourishing, satisfying meals. Without the conveniences of a modern kitchen, understanding the fundamental principles of wilderness cooking becomes essential. Mastering these skills enables you to create varied and flavorful meals that provide the energy and nutrients needed for long-term survival. This chapter delves into key wilderness cooking techniques, including preparing meals over an open fire, building an earth oven for more sophisticated cooking, and preserving food for long-term storage. By learning these methods, you can sustain yourself with confidence and skill in the wild.

PREPARING MEALS OVER AN OPEN FIRE

Cooking over an open fire is one of the oldest and most versatile methods used by humans. It allows for a range of cooking techniques, including boiling, grilling, roasting, and even baking with the right tools and setup. However, preparing meals over an open fire requires a keen understanding of fire management, temperature control, and the efficient use of available resources.

The key to cooking over an open fire is to establish a steady and manageable flame. Building a fire for cooking differs from building one for warmth. For cooking, you aim for a consistent bed of hot coals rather than large, roaring flames. Hot coals provide even heat and can be controlled more easily, making them ideal for grilling and slow cooking.

Types of Fire Structures

Different fire structures suit various cooking methods. For instance, the teepee fire is great for initially building heat but isn't ideal for cooking because its flames are high and erratic. Instead, once you have enough embers, switch to a log cabin fire or star fire, which provides a stable base for placing pots, grilling, or roasting food.

Another method is the trench fire, which involves digging a small trench and building the fire within it. This method allows you to place a spit over the trench for roasting meat or fish. The trench helps control the flame and retains heat, making it a practical option when you need to manage the fire's intensity and direction.

Techniques for Cooking Over the Fire

1. Direct Grilling: Grilling directly over the fire is a straightforward method that works well

for small game, fish, and vegetables. Place a green, non-toxic stick through your food and rest it over the coals, ensuring it rotates for even cooking. For fish, the skin helps protect the meat from burning, while vegetables like onions or tubers can be skewered and cooked similarly.

2. Cooking on Hot Stones: Another ancient technique involves heating flat stones directly in the fire. Once they are hot, remove them and place your food directly on the stone's surface. This method works particularly well for thin cuts of meat, fish fillets, or flatbreads. The stone retains heat, cooking food evenly and imparting a subtle, smoky flavor.

3. Using a Pot or Pan: If you have a pot or pan, open fire cooking expands its versatility. Boiling water for soups, stews, or tea is straightforward over a fire. By hanging the pot on a tripod or placing it on a flat rock within the coals, you control the cooking temperature. Stews are especially effective in the wilderness, allowing you to combine various foraged ingredients—wild greens, small game, edible roots—into a single, nutrient-dense meal. Boiling not only makes tough vegetables edible but also helps extract nutrients and flavors from meat bones and plant material.

Maintaining and Managing Heat

Successful open fire cooking hinges on the ability to manage heat levels. The distance from the flame, the height of the cooking surface, and the type of wood used all play crucial roles. Hardwoods like oak and hickory are ideal for cooking as they burn slower and produce hotter coals, while softwoods burn quickly and are best used to start the fire.

Cooking with indirect heat is another important skill. For example, by placing food beside the fire rather than directly over it, you can slow-cook meat, which makes it more tender. Wrapping vegetables or game in large leaves (such as burdock or grape leaves) and placing them near the embers creates a steaming effect, locking in moisture and flavor while cooking food thoroughly.

BUILDING AN EARTH OVEN FOR COOKING

While open fires are versatile, they can be limiting when it comes to baking or slow-cooking larger meals. In these cases, building an earth oven is an invaluable skill. Earth ovens are ancient cooking structures that use the natural properties of soil and stone to trap heat, providing a controlled and even cooking environment. They are ideal for baking bread, roasting large cuts of meat, or preparing root vegetables in bulk.

Constructing an Earth Oven

Building an earth oven starts with selecting the right location and gathering the necessary materials. You will need stones, clay soil, and plant material (leaves, grass, or moss). Follow these steps to construct a basic earth oven:

1. Dig the Pit: Choose a flat area and dig a pit that is deep and wide enough to fit the food you intend to cook. The size will vary depending on the meal, but a general guideline is about 2-3 feet wide and 1 foot deep for most small game or vegetable dishes.

2. Line the Pit with Stones: Find flat stones and line the bottom and sides of the pit. These stones will absorb and retain heat, ensuring an even cooking temperature throughout. It's essential to use non-porous stones that won't crack or explode when heated.

3. Build the Fire: Build a fire directly in the pit, using hardwood if possible for its superior heat retention. Allow the fire to burn for at least an hour to thoroughly heat the stones. Once the stones are hot and glowing, push the embers aside or remove them to prevent direct burning.
4. Prepare the Food: While the stones are heating, prepare your food by wrapping it in natural leaves, which act as a protective barrier and prevent scorching. This method also adds moisture, effectively steaming the food within its wrap. If leaves are not available, use a clay coating around the food to create a natural shell.
5. Cook the Food: Place the wrapped food on the hot stones. Cover the pit with a layer of leaves or grass, and then mound soil over the top to seal in the heat. The insulated environment allows the food to cook slowly, often taking several hours depending on the size and type of food being prepared. This method is ideal for cooking tougher meats, which become tender with slow, even heat.

Benefits of Using an Earth Oven

The earth oven's primary advantage is its ability to cook food slowly and evenly, which is crucial for tougher meats and starchy vegetables that benefit from extended cooking times. The trapped steam from the leaves or clay wrapping keeps food moist, while the consistent heat cooks it thoroughly, making it a perfect method for large group meals or preserving the flavor and nutrients of freshly foraged ingredients.

Earth ovens are also energy-efficient. Once the initial fire heats the stones, the cooking process requires no additional fuel, allowing you to conserve wood and focus on other tasks while your meal cooks unattended. This method, though time-consuming, is highly effective in providing balanced, nutrient-rich meals in a wilderness setting.

PRESERVING FOOD FOR LONG-TERM STORAGE

In the wilderness, having a consistent and sustainable food source is essential for survival. While fresh food provides immediate nourishment, it's critical to know how to preserve food for long-term storage, especially when facing seasonal changes, migration, or uncertain availability of resources. Traditional preservation methods—such as drying, smoking, and fermenting—extend the shelf life of food, ensuring that you have reserves to draw upon during lean times.

Drying Food

Drying is one of the simplest and most effective ways to preserve food in the wild. It removes moisture, which inhibits the growth of bacteria and mold, making food safe to store for weeks or even months. This technique works well for meat, fish, fruits, and vegetables.

To dry meat (like venison or rabbit), slice it into thin strips and hang it over a frame or branch in the sun. Make sure to choose a spot with good airflow and exposure to sunlight. If the weather is humid or unpredictable, smoke drying can be more effective. For fish, clean and fillet it before hanging it on sticks over a smoky fire. The smoke not only dries the fish but also adds flavor and further protects it from spoilage.

Vegetables and fruits, such as wild berries or mushrooms, can also be dried by placing them on flat rocks or makeshift drying racks exposed to the sun. Turn them periodically to ensure even drying. Once completely dried, store them in sealed pouches made from leaves or bark to keep out moisture.

Smoking Meat and Fish

Smoking is another ancient preservation method that combines drying with the protective properties of smoke. A smoky fire, especially from hardwoods like oak or hickory, imparts flavor while preserving meat. To build a smokehouse, construct a simple frame using sticks, cover it with a tarp or leaves, and create a vent at the top to allow smoke to circulate.

Hang the meat strips or fish fillets inside the structure, and build a low fire beneath, keeping the temperature controlled to avoid cooking the meat directly. Allow the meat to smoke for several hours or even overnight until it becomes firm and dry. Properly smoked food can be stored for weeks and serves as a valuable, lightweight food source when traveling.

Fermenting for Long-Term Storage

Fermentation is a method that preserves and enhances the nutritional value of vegetables and plant material. In the wild, fermenting greens, roots, and even wild grains is possible with minimal equipment. For example, you can ferment cabbage-like greens by packing them into a hollowed-out container and covering them with a salty brine (if salt is available). The process encourages the growth of beneficial bacteria that protect the food from spoilage and provide valuable nutrients.

The fermentation process typically takes several days to weeks, depending on the temperature and the type of plant material used. Once fermented, the food can be stored in cool conditions and consumed over an extended period, providing essential vitamins and minerals during times when fresh vegetables are not available.

COMBINING TECHNIQUES FOR EFFICIENT WILDERNESS COOKING

Mastering these cooking and preservation techniques allows you to adapt and thrive in various wilderness scenarios. By understanding how to prepare meals over an open fire, build and use an earth oven, and preserve food through drying, smoking, and fermenting, you expand your ability to maintain a balanced diet that supports physical health and energy levels.

Incorporating these methods into your survival strategy ensures that you can not only survive but also make the most of the natural resources available. Cooking becomes more than just a necessity; it transforms into an art of utilizing the wilderness sustainably, combining ingenuity with traditional skills to provide nourishment and comfort, regardless of your environment.

BOOK 13
USING IMPROVISED TOOLS AND MATERIALS

In the wilderness, the ability to create and use tools is a critical survival skill. Modern conveniences such as knives, ropes, and cooking utensils are often taken for granted, but when faced with the challenge of living off the land, knowing how to craft these items from natural materials becomes essential. Improvised tools provide the means to build shelter, prepare food, gather resources, and defend yourself. This chapter explores the process of crafting tools from rocks and wood, creating ropes and cords from natural fibers, and making cooking utensils from found materials. By developing these skills, you transform the wilderness from a daunting environment into a resource-rich haven where you can thrive.

CRAFTING TOOLS FROM ROCKS AND WOOD

Rocks and wood are some of the most accessible materials in the wilderness, and when used skillfully, they can be fashioned into effective tools for cutting, digging, building, and hunting. This section delves into the techniques required to craft these tools, emphasizing the importance of selecting the right materials and applying the correct methods.

Selecting Suitable Rocks

The first step in making tools from rocks is understanding the types of rocks available. Not all rocks are suitable for toolmaking; the ideal choices are those that are hard and brittle, such as flint, chert, quartzite, or basalt. These rocks fracture in a predictable manner, making it possible to shape them into sharp edges. The process of flintknapping, an ancient technique used by indigenous cultures, involves striking rocks at specific angles to produce sharp flakes that can be used as blades or arrowheads.

To create a basic cutting tool, find a suitable piece of flint or chert and another hard stone, known as a hammerstone. Use the hammerstone to strike the flint at a slight angle, chipping off sharp flakes. These flakes can be used as immediate cutting tools, while the larger core can be shaped into more refined tools like hand axes or scrapers. The sharp edges produced by flintknapping are ideal for cutting ropes, carving wood, and processing game.

Making a Stone Axe

A stone axe is a versatile tool useful for chopping wood, digging, and even defending yourself. To create one, find a large, flat rock with a sharp edge and a sturdy piece of wood for the handle. The rock should be hard enough to withstand repeated impacts but not so brittle that it shatters easily.

1. Carve a Notch in the Wood: Carve a notch into one end of the wooden handle where the stone axe head will be secured. This notch should be deep enough to hold the stone securely.
2. Attach the Stone Head: Place the stone in the notch and wrap it tightly with cordage (which you can create from natural fibers, as discussed later in this chapter). Ensure the stone is firmly held in place to prevent it from coming loose during use.
3. Reinforce with Adhesive: If you have access to resin or pine sap, use it to glue the stone in place. These natural adhesives harden when dry, providing additional stability to the axe head.

With a stone axe, you can chop wood for shelter, process game, and fashion other tools, making it a cornerstone of improvised toolmaking.

Carving and Shaping Wood

Wood is abundant and can be crafted into a variety of tools. Hardwoods like oak, hickory, and ash are ideal for making sturdy implements, while softwoods such as pine are better for crafting items that require less strength but more flexibility. To work with wood effectively, it's important to have a sharp stone knife or axe.

Spears and Digging Sticks: Spears are essential for hunting and defense. To make a spear, find a straight branch from a hardwood tree and carve one end into a sharp point using a stone blade. To harden the tip, briefly hold it over a fire, rotating it until it becomes charred and firm. This process strengthens the wood, making it more resistant to breaking.

Digging sticks are simple yet effective tools for uprooting edible roots, digging fire pits, or turning soil. To create one, select a sturdy branch, sharpen one end, and smooth the handle for comfortable use. A digging stick is a versatile tool that serves as a primitive shovel in a variety of survival scenarios.

Bow Drill for Fire Making: Crafting a bow drill is another essential skill for making fire without modern tools. You'll need a straight, sturdy stick (the spindle), a flat piece of wood (the fireboard), and a curved branch (the bow). The bow is strung with cordage (which can be made from natural fibers). The spindle is placed in a notch in the fireboard and is rotated rapidly using the bow's sawing motion. This creates friction, producing an ember that can be used to start a fire. The bow drill is a prime example of using wood effectively in the wilderness to solve a critical survival need.

CREATING ROPES AND CORDS FROM NATURAL FIBERS

Cordage is one of the most useful items in the wilderness, essential for building shelters, setting traps, securing tools, and even making fire. Without access to synthetic ropes, you must rely on natural fibers to create strong, reliable cordage. Fortunately, the wilderness offers a variety of plants and trees that provide suitable materials for rope making.

Identifying Fiber-Rich Plants

To create effective cordage, you need to identify plants that offer strong, flexible fibers. Some of the best options include:

- Yucca: Found in arid regions, the leaves of the yucca plant contain strong fibers that can be stripped and twisted into cordage.
- Cattail: Common in wetland areas, cattail leaves can be split into long, narrow strips and dried for use in rope making.
- Nettle: A plant with fibrous stems, nettle requires careful handling (to avoid stings), but its fibers are extremely durable when processed properly.
- Inner Bark of Trees: Trees like basswood, willow, and cedar have inner bark that can be peeled off and used as cordage. This bark is strong and can be twisted or braided to create sturdy ropes.

Processing Natural Fibers

Once you've identified suitable plants, the next step is processing the fibers. For plants like cattails or yucca, strip the leaves into narrow strands. Dry them in the sun to remove moisture, making the fibers easier to work with. For nettle, cut the stems and peel away the outer layer to access the inner fibers. Allow these fibers to dry, then soak them briefly in water to soften them before twisting.

Twisting Cordage

The most basic method of making cordage is twisting. Start with two fibers of equal length. Hold one end of both strands together, and twist each fiber tightly in the same direction (clockwise). Once they are tightly twisted, wrap them around each other in the opposite direction (counterclockwise). This process, known as the reverse wrap, creates a strong and flexible rope. Continue adding fibers as needed to increase the length, ensuring that new fibers are spliced seamlessly into the twist.

For a stronger rope, braid multiple strands together or create a three-ply twist, which involves twisting three strands simultaneously. The tighter and more consistent the twist, the stronger and more durable the cordage will be.

Applications of Natural Cordage

Cordage can be used in countless ways in the wilderness:

- Building Shelters: Strong cords are essential for lashing branches together when constructing shelters like lean-tos or debris huts.
- Making Bowstrings: When hunting, a bowstring made from plant fibers or animal sinew can be used to string a primitive bow.
- Fishing Lines and Nets: Thinner cordage is perfect for crafting fishing lines or weaving nets for trapping fish in streams and shallow waters.
- Setting Traps: Snares require durable cordage that can withstand the struggle of captured animals. Twisting or braiding your cordage increases its strength and resilience for this purpose.

MAKING COOKING UTENSILS FROM FOUND MATERIALS

Preparing food in the wilderness often requires improvised utensils. Crafting cooking tools from wood, stone, or bone allows you to create functional items like spoons, bowls, and tongs. These tools not only improve your cooking capabilities but also enhance the variety and quality of meals you can prepare.

Crafting Wooden Utensils

Wood is the most accessible material for making cooking utensils. To craft a simple spoon, start with a piece of hardwood that is about the length of your hand and wide enough to carve into. Using a stone knife or a flake, carve out a shallow bowl shape at one end of the wood, then shape the handle by whittling down the opposite end. The process requires patience and precision, but the result is a sturdy spoon that can be used for stirring, serving, or eating.

Creating Wooden Bowls

To create a wooden bowl, you'll need a larger piece of wood. Hollow out the center using hot coals from your fire and a small stone tool to scrape away the charred wood. This method, known as coal burning, allows you to control the depth and shape of the bowl without advanced tools. The result is a functional container that can hold water, food, or other essentials.

Making Bone and Shell Utensils

If you have access to bones from hunted animals or shells from riverbeds, these materials can also be repurposed into useful tools. Long bones, such as those from deer or rabbits, can be split lengthwise to create flat surfaces that work well as knives or spatulas. Sand down the edges with rough stones to smooth the surfaces and sharpen the ends.

Shells, on the other hand, are ideal for scooping and scraping. Large shells can be used as makeshift ladles or even plates, while smaller ones serve as scoops for transferring hot coals or embers when cooking.

Making Tongs and Grills

When cooking over an open fire, having tools to handle hot items is essential. Tongs can be crafted from a split branch, using its natural springiness to grip and move hot stones, embers, or pieces of meat. Simply find a forked stick, cut one side partially to create a hinge-like effect, and sand the tips smooth for better grip.

Grills can also be improvised by weaving green branches into a grid pattern. The branches should be non-toxic and freshly cut to prevent burning. This grid can then be placed over a fire pit, creating a surface to cook fish, meat, or flatbreads directly over the coals.

COMBINING TOOLS AND MATERIALS FOR COMPLEX PROJECTS

As you become proficient in crafting basic tools and utensils, you can begin to combine materials and techniques for more complex projects. For example, a simple smoker can be built by constructing a frame from sticks and covering it with bark or leaves. Hang meat or fish inside the structure, then use a slow, smoky fire underneath to preserve your catch.

Another advanced project is crafting a hunting bow. This requires selecting a flexible but strong branch (like hickory or yew), carving it into the appropriate shape, and using your hand-twisted cordage for the bowstring. Arrows can be fashioned from straight shoots of wood, with stone arrowheads and feather fletching for stability in flight. Combining these elements not only enhances your hunting capabilities but also demonstrates the power of mastering multiple skills in survival toolmaking.

CONCLUSION

Using improvised tools and materials is a fundamental survival skill that transforms the wilderness into a place of opportunity rather than hardship. By learning to craft tools from rocks and wood, creating reliable cordage from natural fibers, and making functional cooking utensils, you gain the ability to build, hunt, cook, and sustain yourself effectively in any environment. These skills empower you to interact with nature in a way that is both resourceful and respectful, ensuring that you can thrive even when modern conveniences are out of reach.

BOOK 14

DRONES FOR WILDERNESS SURVEILLANCE

Drones, also known as Unmanned Aerial Vehicles (UAVs), have revolutionized the way we explore and interact with remote environments. In wilderness survival, drones offer unparalleled opportunities for surveillance, mapping, and resource monitoring. These devices extend your vision beyond the immediate landscape, allowing you to navigate unknown territories, identify resources, and monitor environmental changes with minimal physical effort. While traditionally associated with technology-dependent lifestyles, drones can be effectively integrated into wilderness survival to enhance safety and efficiency. This chapter covers the fundamentals of setting up and controlling drones in the wilderness, using drone technology for terrain mapping, and monitoring natural resources to maximize their potential in long-term survival situations.

SETTING UP AND CONTROLLING DRONES IN THE WILDERNESS

Operating a drone in the wilderness differs significantly from using one in urban or suburban settings. The absence of infrastructure, like reliable power sources and stable GPS signals, requires careful preparation and understanding of the drone's capabilities. To effectively utilize drones in remote environments, it is essential to master their setup and operation.

Choosing the Right Drone for Wilderness Use

Selecting the right drone is the first step in ensuring its effectiveness in a wilderness setting. The ideal drone for survival scenarios should be rugged, portable, and capable of long flight times. Look for models that are weather-resistant, as they need to withstand varying conditions such as rain, wind, or extreme temperatures. Additionally, the drone should have long battery life or support for external battery packs to extend its operational time in the field. Drones with modular components are also advantageous, as they allow for the replacement of damaged parts and attachment of additional accessories like cameras or thermal sensors.

Compact, foldable drones are particularly suitable for wilderness surveillance due to their portability. They are easy to pack and deploy quickly, making them efficient tools for immediate reconnaissance missions.

Power Management and Charging in Remote Locations

One of the biggest challenges of using drones in the wilderness is maintaining power. Drones rely on batteries, and when used intensively, these can drain quickly. A typical drone battery may last anywhere from 20 to 40 minutes, so bringing multiple charged batteries is essential. However, when you're far from a power grid, recharging these batteries requires careful planning.

Portable solar panels are an ideal solution for recharging batteries in the wilderness. Set up a solar charging station during daylight hours, ensuring the panels are positioned for maximum sun exposure. Additionally, power banks capable of multiple recharges can be used as backup energy sources, ensuring that you always have a charged battery ready for the next flight.

Another option is using a hand-crank generator for emergency recharging. Although it requires manual effort, this method can provide enough power to recharge small batteries, making it a viable backup when solar or other power sources are unavailable.

Calibrating the Drone

Before launching the drone, it's crucial to calibrate its compass and GPS systems, especially in a wilderness environment where magnetic fields or interference from natural elements might affect performance. Most modern drones have automatic calibration processes, which involve rotating the drone horizontally and vertically to align its sensors. Conduct this calibration in an open space, away from large metal objects or rock formations that could interfere with the compass readings.

Additionally, test the signal strength and make sure the drone's software is updated with the latest firmware. This ensures that any bugs or malfunctions are minimized and that the drone operates optimally during flight. Ensuring a strong and stable connection between the drone and its controller is vital, especially when flying over long distances or difficult terrains. Drones equipped with obstacle avoidance technology are particularly valuable in wilderness settings, as they can autonomously navigate around trees, cliffs, and other obstacles, reducing the risk of crashes.

Controlling the Drone and Monitoring Flight Conditions

Understanding the drone's flight controls and monitoring environmental conditions are key to successful operations. The wilderness presents several challenges, such as wind gusts, altitude changes, and weather variability, all of which can affect flight performance.

When launching the drone, choose a clear, open space with minimal obstructions. Avoid areas with thick foliage or rugged terrain that could interfere with takeoff or landing. Keep a close eye on the weather, particularly wind speed. While drones are designed to operate in mild wind conditions, high winds can destabilize them or drain the battery faster as they work to maintain stability. Flying in extreme cold or heat can also affect battery life and performance, so always consider these factors before flight.

Flying drones at higher altitudes requires careful control of battery usage and monitoring of GPS signals. High-altitude flights offer extensive views of the terrain but can also be risky if battery levels are low, as the drone needs enough power to descend and return safely.

MAPPING TERRAIN USING DRONE TECHNOLOGY

Drones are invaluable tools for mapping large areas quickly and efficiently. They provide aerial perspectives that are impossible to achieve from the ground, enabling you to scout vast regions, plot routes, and identify potential hazards or resources. By understanding how to use drones for mapping, you can create accurate terrain models that aid navigation and enhance your survival strategies.

Using Camera Technology for Mapping

Most drones come equipped with high-resolution cameras capable of capturing detailed aerial images. When mapping terrain, fly the drone at a consistent altitude and speed to ensure that the images captured are evenly spaced and overlap sufficiently. Overlapping images are essential for creating a cohesive map, as they allow software programs to stitch together multiple photos, forming a panoramic view of the terrain.

If your drone supports it, geotagging photos—where each image is marked with GPS coordinates—can significantly enhance the mapping process. Geotagged photos are especially useful for tracking your location in unfamiliar territory. By reviewing these photos later, you can identify key landmarks, water sources, or campsites, and plot them accurately on a map.

Creating 3D Terrain Models

Advanced drones equipped with LIDAR (Light Detection and Ranging) or 3D mapping software can generate highly detailed terrain models. These models allow you to visualize the landscape's contours, elevations, and features. Using software like DroneDeploy or Pix4D, you can input your drone's flight data and aerial photos to create 3D maps. These models provide valuable information about elevation changes, slope gradients, and vegetation density, which are critical for planning routes and locating optimal sites for shelter or resources.

In cases where such advanced equipment is not available, drones can still provide valuable topographical images by taking overlapping photos at different altitudes and angles. You can use these images to manually draw or sketch a map of the area, noting important features like rivers, ridgelines, or valleys. This manual approach, while less precise, is still a powerful tool for understanding your surroundings and planning your movements.

Flight Path Planning for Effective Mapping

To map a large area effectively, planning the drone's flight path is essential. Use grid patterns or zigzag routes to cover a specific area comprehensively. By programming the drone to follow a systematic flight path, you ensure that no part of the landscape is missed and that the images collected are consistent.

Modern drones often have waypoint navigation features, allowing you to set specific coordinates and program the drone to fly autonomously between these points. This feature is particularly useful when mapping areas with challenging terrain or regions that are otherwise inaccessible. Waypoint navigation also conserves battery power by optimizing the drone's flight efficiency, enabling you to map larger areas on a single charge.

Analyzing and Interpreting Drone Maps

Once you have collected aerial imagery, the next step is analyzing the data to interpret the terrain and extract useful information. Look for natural barriers, such as cliffs or dense forests, and mark them on your map as areas to avoid. Conversely, open spaces, clearings, or areas near water sources should be noted as potential campsites or resource hubs.

If the terrain appears varied, with steep elevation changes, use the drone imagery to assess routes that follow natural contours. This reduces the risk of exhaustion or injury from climbing and descending steep slopes unnecessarily. In open areas, identify landmarks like large rocks, distinctive tree lines, or bodies of water that can serve as visual guides during your journey.

By combining drone mapping with traditional navigation skills, such as using a compass and reading topographical features from the ground, you create a multi-layered understanding of the wilderness environment, enhancing your ability to navigate safely and effectively.

MONITORING NATURAL RESOURCES WITH DRONES

One of the most significant advantages of drones in a wilderness context is their ability to monitor natural resources over large areas. Whether you're tracking wildlife, locating water sources, or assessing plant growth, drones provide a bird's-eye view that extends your capacity to gather information and make informed survival decisions.

Locating Water Sources

Water is one of the most critical resources in the wilderness, and finding it can mean the difference between survival and hardship. Drones, with their aerial perspective, allow you to scan large areas for signs of water, such as riverbeds, ponds, and lakes. Look for clusters of green vegetation or changes in terrain that indicate moisture. In arid environments, drones can spot hidden water sources like desert springs or oases that might not be visible from the ground.

Monitoring Wildlife Movements

Tracking wildlife is crucial for securing food and understanding the ecosystem you are navigating. Drones equipped with thermal imaging can detect animals' heat signatures even in dense forests or at night. By flying the drone over likely habitats, such as clearings, waterholes, or trails, you can observe patterns of movement, identify species, and plan hunting strategies accordingly.

Drones also allow you to monitor the health and behavior of wildlife without disturbing them. For example, by observing animals' migration patterns or the presence of specific species, you gain insight into seasonal changes, potential dangers (such as predator activity), and areas where resources like food might be concentrated.

Assessing Vegetation and Foraging Opportunities

Identifying areas rich in vegetation is essential for locating edible plants and resources for shelter. Drones provide an efficient way to scan large areas for these opportunities. Look for patches of green, particularly near water sources or low-lying areas where moisture accumulates. Use drone imagery to differentiate between dense forests, open meadows, and brushlands, helping you determine where specific types of plants are likely to grow.

Foraging becomes more strategic when you have an aerial view of the area, as you can plan routes that pass through areas with high concentrations of edible plants or other useful resources. This approach minimizes energy expenditure and increases efficiency, which is critical when you need to sustain yourself in the wilderness.

Surveying Weather Patterns and Environmental Changes

Drones equipped with cameras can also be used to monitor weather patterns and environmental changes, providing crucial information for survival planning. By flying drones to higher altitudes, you can observe cloud formations, wind patterns, and the movement of weather fronts. This information is valuable for predicting storms, monitoring fire risks (such as spotting smoke plumes), and assessing the safety of routes in mountainous or coastal regions prone to sudden weather shifts.

Additionally, drones can be used to track the spread of wildfires or floods, helping you identify safe zones and escape routes. The ability to gather this kind of real-time data from an aerial perspective ensures that you can react quickly and avoid potentially life-threatening situations.

INTEGRATING DRONES WITH TRADITIONAL SURVIVAL SKILLS

While drones offer incredible advantages in wilderness survival, it's important to remember that they are tools meant to complement, not replace, traditional skills. Drones depend on technology, power sources, and clear weather conditions, all of which can be unreliable in the wilderness. Therefore, mastering skills such as reading natural landmarks, using a compass, and building shelter remain essential.

By integrating drones into your overall survival strategy, you create a robust system that leverages technology while maintaining the versatility and reliability of traditional wilderness skills. For instance, drones can map an area and identify resources, while a compass and mental mapping skills ensure that you can navigate even when technology fails. This multi-faceted approach enhances your ability to adapt and survive in any environment.

CONCLUSION

Drones are powerful tools that expand your capabilities in the wilderness, providing surveillance, mapping, and resource monitoring that would otherwise be impossible. By mastering their setup and operation, learning how to map terrain effectively, and using drones to monitor natural resources, you can navigate and survive more efficiently in remote environments. While technology enhances these capabilities, it is crucial to blend drone skills with traditional survival techniques, ensuring that you are prepared for any scenario nature presents.

BOOK 15
OFFLINE DIGITAL TOOLS FOR SURVIVAL

In today's digital age, technology offers a vast array of tools that can enhance your survival skills, even when you're deep in the wilderness and disconnected from the internet. Offline digital tools, such as survival apps, GPS devices, and digital notebooks, provide valuable resources that can aid in navigation, resource identification, emergency preparedness, and more. These tools are particularly effective when used alongside traditional survival skills, offering a modern advantage in an otherwise primitive environment. This chapter covers the top survival apps for offline use, integrating GPS and map tools without internet access, and utilizing digital notebooks for wilderness journaling, ensuring you can maximize the benefits of technology even in the most remote locations.

TOP SURVIVAL APPS FOR OFFLINE USE

While the internet may not be accessible in the wilderness, many apps are specifically designed to work offline, providing crucial information when you need it most. These apps offer everything from navigation aids to plant identification and first aid instructions, turning your smartphone into a multi-functional survival device. Knowing which apps to download and how to use them effectively is essential for enhancing your wilderness skills.

1. Offline Topographic Maps (e.g., Gaia GPS, AllTrails)

Apps like Gaia GPS and AllTrails are invaluable tools for navigation. They allow you to download topographic maps before heading into the wilderness, so you can access them even without an internet connection. These maps provide detailed information on elevation changes, terrain features, trails, and landmarks, making them essential for route planning and orienteering.

Before heading out, download maps of the area you plan to explore. You can save these maps at various zoom levels, from broad overviews of large regions to detailed views of specific trails. By using your device's built-in GPS, these apps can pinpoint your location on the map, helping you navigate in real-time even when there's no cellular signal.

2. First Aid Guides (e.g., Red Cross First Aid)

In the wilderness, accidents happen, and being prepared to handle them is crucial. Red Cross First Aid and other similar apps provide comprehensive offline guides for treating injuries, from minor cuts and burns to more serious emergencies like fractures or hypothermia. These apps include step-by-step instructions, visual guides, and even videos that can be accessed without internet, ensuring that you have life-saving information at your fingertips when needed.

Downloading an offline first aid guide before your trip is a proactive step that ensures you're prepared for the unexpected. It's essential to familiarize yourself with the app's interface and content ahead of time, so you know where to find information quickly during an emergency.

3. Plant Identification (e.g., PlantNet, PictureThis)

Knowing which plants are edible, medicinal, or dangerous is a critical survival skill. Apps like PlantNet and PictureThis allow you to take photos of plants and identify them based on a database that includes thousands of species. While these apps typically work better with internet access, you can still use their offline functions by downloading plant libraries relevant to your area.

These apps provide information about plant uses, from nutritional value to medicinal properties. By using them offline, you can safely forage for food and medicine, significantly enhancing your self-reliance. It's important to download the plant databases for the regions you plan to explore and practice using the app before heading out, ensuring you're comfortable with the identification process.

4. Survival Guides (e.g., SAS Survival Guide)

The SAS Survival Guide app is a digital version of one of the most trusted survival manuals. It provides a comprehensive collection of tips and instructions on building shelters, finding water, starting fires, and signaling for rescue. The offline capability allows you to access all this information without needing a network connection, making it a powerful tool for anyone venturing into remote areas.

Having an app like this on your phone acts as a portable survival encyclopedia, giving you access to critical information when you need it most. It's advisable to explore the app's contents before your trip, so you know what sections are available and can easily navigate to the information you need in a crisis.

5. Weather and Environment Monitoring (e.g., MyRadar, Windy)

While weather apps typically rely on internet connections for real-time updates, some, like MyRadar and Windy, allow you to download weather data and maps for offline access. By doing so, you can track weather patterns, predict changes, and prepare for storms or extreme conditions before they hit.

Before venturing into the wilderness, download the latest weather data and maps. These apps can display wind patterns, temperature changes, and pressure systems, helping you anticipate weather shifts and adapt your plans accordingly. Understanding how to interpret this data offline can be a crucial aspect of staying safe and avoiding hazardous conditions.

INTEGRATING GPS AND MAP TOOLS WITHOUT INTERNET

GPS technology is a game-changer for wilderness navigation, offering precise location tracking even in the most remote areas. By integrating GPS with offline map tools, you can navigate confidently without relying on cellular networks or internet connections. Understanding how to use GPS devices and offline maps effectively ensures that you can find your way through challenging terrains and unfamiliar landscapes.

Understanding How GPS Works Offline

GPS operates independently of cellular networks by using signals from satellites orbiting the Earth. This means that as long as your device has GPS capability, it can determine your location even without an internet connection. However, it's crucial to prepare your device properly for offline use to maximize its functionality.

Downloading Maps for Offline Access

The key to using GPS offline is to download maps in advance. Apps like Gaia GPS, Google Maps, and Maps.me allow you to save maps for offline use. Before heading into the wilderness, plan your route and download the relevant map sections, ensuring that you have both broad overviews and detailed zoom levels. This provides flexibility in navigation, allowing you to check both your overall progress and specific trail conditions.

Using Waypoints and Routes

Once you have the maps downloaded, set waypoints and plan routes before your trip. Waypoints are specific coordinates or locations (such as campsites, water sources, or significant landmarks) that you can mark on your map. These markers guide you along your path, ensuring that you stay on track even when the terrain is unfamiliar.

Routes, on the other hand, are planned paths that connect multiple waypoints. By plotting a route before your journey, you can see the overall distance, elevation changes, and estimated travel time. As you travel, your GPS device will track your progress in real-time, helping you adjust your pace and confirm your position relative to your planned route.

Using GPS Devices and Smartphones in Tandem

While smartphones offer convenience and versatility, dedicated GPS devices, like Garmin units, are often more reliable in remote areas. They are built to withstand rugged conditions, have longer battery life, and provide more precise data. Using a dedicated GPS alongside your smartphone creates a backup system: if one device fails, you still have a reliable navigation tool available.

Make sure to familiarize yourself with the GPS device's functions, such as marking waypoints, tracking paths, and accessing pre-loaded maps. Practice using these features in familiar terrain before relying on them in a wilderness setting.

Battery Management and Power Solutions

GPS functionality, particularly when used continuously, can drain your device's battery quickly. To manage power effectively, use GPS sparingly, turning it on only when needed. You can also set the device to track mode, which periodically checks your position instead of constantly updating, saving battery life.

Having backup power sources is crucial. Portable solar chargers are ideal for recharging your devices in the wilderness, as they provide a sustainable energy source during daylight hours. Alternatively, power banks with multiple recharges offer reliable support during extended trips, ensuring that your GPS remains operational.

DIGITAL NOTEBOOKS FOR WILDERNESS JOURNALING

Journaling and record-keeping are essential practices for survivalists, helping you document information about routes, resources, weather patterns, wildlife behavior, and plant identification. While traditional pen-and-paper methods work well, digital notebooks offer significant advantages, such as unlimited space, searchable entries, and the ability to store photos and videos. By using apps designed for offline note-taking, you can efficiently organize and access crucial data.

Choosing the Right Digital Notebook App

Several apps are designed to function offline, making them perfect for wilderness journaling. Evernote, Microsoft OneNote, and Google Keep all offer robust features that allow you to create and store notes, images, and even voice memos without internet access. By downloading these apps and preparing them for offline use, you turn your smartphone or tablet into a digital journal that can hold extensive information about your journey.

Structuring Your Digital Journal for Efficiency

To make the most of your digital notebook, organize it in a way that aligns with your survival needs. Create sections or notebooks dedicated to specific categories, such as:

- Routes and Maps: Record details about the trails you plan to take, including waypoints, elevation changes, and potential hazards. Include GPS coordinates and photos of landmarks to help you stay oriented.

- Foraging and Plant Identification: Document the plants you encounter, including photos, descriptions, and notes on edibility or medicinal use. By keeping this information organized, you can reference it quickly in future foraging trips.

- Weather and Environmental Observations: Track weather patterns, wind directions, and temperature changes. This information helps you anticipate shifts in weather and plan accordingly. Recording these details over time also builds a valuable knowledge base for understanding the region's climate patterns.

- Wildlife Behavior and Tracking: Keep notes on animal sightings, tracks, and behavior. This helps you identify areas where animals are likely to gather, aiding in hunting or wildlife observation efforts.

Recording and Storing Visual Data

A significant advantage of digital notebooks is the ability to include photos, videos, and audio recordings alongside written entries. This feature is particularly valuable for plant identification and terrain mapping, as you can capture images of specific plants or landscape features and annotate them directly in your journal.

Photos of landmarks help confirm your location when navigating unfamiliar areas, while recordings of animal sounds or environmental observations provide additional context that may be useful later. For example, recording the call of a bird you encounter frequently can help you locate that species in the future by listening for its distinct sound.

Keeping Notes Organized and Accessible

When using a digital notebook, it's crucial to keep your entries organized and easy to navigate. Utilize tags and labels to categorize your notes. For instance, tag entries related to plant identification with keywords like "edible," "toxic," or "medicinal." This system allows you to quickly filter and find relevant information when you need it.

Regularly backup your notebook to a secondary storage device, such as an SD card or a portable hard drive. Even though you are using digital tools, it's important to safeguard your data, especially when it contains critical survival information.

INTEGRATING OFFLINE DIGITAL TOOLS WITH TRADITIONAL SKILLS

While offline digital tools provide significant advantages, it is essential to remember that they are not infallible. Batteries can drain, devices can be damaged, and software can malfunction. Therefore, these tools should complement—not replace—traditional survival skills.

For example, use offline maps and GPS as supplements to your compass and physical map-reading skills. Practice estimating distances and navigating by natural landmarks so that you are not entirely dependent on digital aids. Similarly, while plant identification apps can be invaluable, develop your botanical knowledge by studying plants and learning to identify them without technology.

Combining Digital and Analog Journaling

Maintaining a physical journal alongside your digital one is a wise practice. The physical journal can serve as a backup, recording essential information such as emergency contacts, waypoints, and survival checklists. This way, if your digital tools fail, you still have a reliable record of vital data.

CONCLUSION

Offline digital tools have the potential to enhance wilderness survival significantly by providing critical information, aiding navigation, and offering resources for emergency situations. By utilizing apps for offline mapping, first aid, plant identification, and note-taking, you expand your capabilities in remote areas where traditional methods may fall short. However, integrating these tools with traditional survival skills is essential for building a balanced approach that ensures preparedness in any scenario. Mastering the use of offline technology while maintaining proficiency in analog skills transforms you into a versatile and adaptable wilderness expert, prepared to navigate and thrive in the most challenging environments.

BOOK 16
MENTAL AND EMOTIONAL STRENGTH

Surviving in the wilderness requires more than just physical skills and knowledge of the environment. One of the most critical aspects of long-term survival is the ability to maintain mental and emotional strength. Isolation, loneliness, stress, and the challenges of navigating an unpredictable environment can weigh heavily on the mind, even for the most experienced survivalist. Developing strategies to manage these psychological aspects is essential for maintaining focus, staying motivated, and ultimately ensuring survival. This chapter explores techniques for managing isolation and loneliness, coping mechanisms for stressful situations, and methods for staying motivated and positive over time.

TECHNIQUES FOR MANAGING ISOLATION AND LONELINESS

Isolation and loneliness are some of the most difficult challenges to overcome when surviving in the wilderness for extended periods. Humans are inherently social beings, and prolonged isolation can lead to emotional distress, disorientation, and even depression. To combat these effects, it is important to cultivate a resilient mindset and develop strategies that keep the mind engaged and emotionally balanced.

Establishing Routines and Structure

Creating a daily routine is one of the most effective ways to manage isolation. A structured schedule provides a sense of purpose and order, helping you maintain focus and avoid feelings of aimlessness that can arise when alone for long periods. Break your day into segments that include essential survival activities such as gathering firewood, foraging, hunting, maintaining shelter, and preparing food. Incorporate time for physical exercise, which not only strengthens your body but also releases endorphins that improve your mood.

When your day has structure, it becomes easier to maintain a rhythm that keeps your mind active and your body moving. Even simple routines, like stretching in the morning, checking the condition of your shelter, or making tea from foraged herbs, help create a sense of normalcy in an otherwise unfamiliar environment. These small habits become anchors that stabilize your mental state, giving you something familiar to look forward to each day.

Engaging in Mental Exercises

The mind, like the body, requires exercise to stay sharp and resilient. Engaging in mental exercises helps stave off the negative effects of isolation and loneliness by keeping your brain active and engaged. These exercises can include memory challenges, mental puzzles, or even practicing survival scenarios in your mind.

One technique is to recall and memorize routes you have taken or landmarks you've seen, creating a mental map of your environment. This practice not only sharpens your memory but also builds a mental image of your surroundings that aids navigation and familiarity with the area.

Another method is practicing visualization. Visualization is the process of creating vivid mental images of positive memories, loved ones, or future goals. Visualizing yourself successfully completing tasks or reaching safety can boost motivation and reinforce the belief that you are capable of overcoming your current challenges. Imagining conversations with friends or loved ones also provides a sense of connection, reducing feelings of loneliness.

Using Nature as a Companion

Finding connection and solace in nature is a powerful way to combat isolation. Viewing nature not as a hostile or indifferent force but as a companion can foster a sense of belonging and reduce feelings of loneliness. Observe the patterns of wildlife, the changing weather, the growth of plants, and the rhythms of the natural world around you. By becoming familiar with these cycles, you create a sense of connection that reinforces your place within the environment.

Interacting with nature through mindful practices can also be beneficial. Journaling about your experiences, describing the beauty of a sunset, or noting the sound of the wind through the trees helps you process your emotions and stay grounded. These acts of observation and reflection turn isolation into an opportunity for deeper appreciation and understanding of the environment, fostering a sense of companionship rather than loneliness.

COPING MECHANISMS FOR STRESSFUL SITUATIONS

Stress is an inevitable part of survival, especially in the unpredictable and often unforgiving conditions of the wilderness. Learning how to manage stress effectively is crucial, as it can cloud judgment, impair decision-making, and lead to panic. Developing reliable coping mechanisms helps maintain a clear mind, enabling you to make rational and effective decisions even in high-pressure situations.

Breathing Techniques and Meditation

When faced with stress, the body's natural response is to enter a state of heightened alertness—often referred to as the fight-or-flight response. While this can be beneficial in short bursts, prolonged stress can lead to anxiety, fatigue, and decreased mental clarity. Controlled breathing techniques and meditation are effective ways to counteract these effects, activating the body's relaxation response.

One simple breathing technique is box breathing, which involves inhaling for four counts, holding the breath for four counts, exhaling for four counts, and holding again for four counts before repeating the cycle. This method slows the heart rate and promotes a sense of calm, helping you regain control of your emotions during stressful situations. Practicing this regularly also improves your ability to manage stress when it arises unexpectedly.

Progressive Muscle Relaxation (PMR) is another technique that can help relieve tension and stress. This involves tensing and then slowly releasing each muscle group in the body, starting from the toes and working your way up to the head. By consciously focusing on each part of your body, you divert attention from stressors, encouraging physical and mental relaxation.

Acceptance and Grounding Techniques

Stressful situations in the wilderness often stem from factors beyond your control, such as severe weather, limited resources, or the presence of dangerous wildlife. A powerful coping mechanism is the practice of acceptance, which involves acknowledging the reality of your circumstances without becoming overwhelmed by fear or frustration. Acceptance does not mean resignation; rather, it is the recognition of the situation as it is, allowing you to respond rationally and with focus.

Grounding techniques are also effective for reducing stress, particularly when emotions start to feel overwhelming. Grounding involves connecting with the present moment and your immediate surroundings. For example, take a moment to focus on what you can see, hear, and feel—the texture of the earth beneath your feet, the sound of birds, the sight of the trees swaying in the wind. This mindfulness practice helps you stay present and reduces the sense of panic or anxiety that can arise when your mind fixates on worst-case scenarios.

Problem-Solving Approach

In the wilderness, many stressors stem from practical problems, such as finding food, building shelter, or navigating unknown terrain. Approaching these challenges with a problem-solving mindset transforms stress into a manageable and constructive process. Break down each issue into smaller, actionable steps rather than viewing it as one overwhelming task.

For instance, if you are struggling to find a reliable water source, start by identifying areas where water might be present, such as low-lying valleys, animal trails, or places where vegetation is lush. Prioritize which locations to explore first and systematically check each option. By focusing on specific actions, you take control of the situation, reducing feelings of helplessness and boosting confidence in your abilities.

STAYING MOTIVATED AND POSITIVE OVER TIME

Maintaining motivation and a positive outlook is critical for long-term survival. As days turn into weeks or months, it's easy to feel worn down by the physical and emotional demands of wilderness living. Developing strategies to keep your spirits high and your mind focused on goals is essential for overcoming fatigue and remaining proactive in your survival efforts.

Setting Short-Term and Long-Term Goals

One of the most effective ways to stay motivated is by setting both short-term and long-term goals. Short-term goals provide immediate, achievable targets that keep you focused and give a sense of accomplishment. These goals can be as simple as gathering enough firewood for the night, catching a fish, or exploring a new area for potential resources. Achieving these smaller tasks reinforces a sense of progress and purpose.

Long-term goals, on the other hand, provide direction and keep your mind focused on the broader picture. These might include finding a more secure shelter location before winter, building a water collection system, or gradually expanding your knowledge of edible plants in the area. By combining short-term and long-term objectives, you create a dynamic framework that keeps you engaged and driven, helping you look beyond the immediate challenges.

Using Positive Self-Talk and Affirmations

Your internal dialogue plays a significant role in shaping your mental state and motivation. In survival situations, it's easy to slip into negative self-talk, especially when faced with setbacks or difficulties. However, positive self-talk can counteract these tendencies and boost your resilience. Reminding yourself of past successes, repeating affirmations like "I am capable" or "I have the skills to survive," and reinforcing the idea that challenges are opportunities for growth can shift your mindset and improve your outlook.

When self-doubt or fear begins to surface, actively challenge those thoughts. Replace "I can't handle this" with "I have handled challenges before, and I will handle this too." By consciously changing your thought patterns, you build mental strength and fortify your resilience against stress and adversity.

Engaging in Creative and Enjoyable Activities

Finding joy and satisfaction in small activities is an important aspect of staying positive over time. In the wilderness, engaging in creative tasks like crafting tools, building decorative elements for your shelter, or writing and sketching in a journal can provide a sense of accomplishment and mental stimulation. These activities, while seemingly minor, offer an outlet for self-expression and a way to break up the monotony of survival tasks.

Connecting with the Environment

A positive outlook is also nurtured through a connection with the natural world. Spending time observing wildlife, exploring new areas, or simply sitting quietly to appreciate the beauty of your surroundings can renew your spirit and provide a sense of peace. Developing a gratitude practice, where you acknowledge the positive aspects of each day, helps maintain a balanced perspective. Even small moments, like witnessing a sunrise or finding a new source of food, become sources of encouragement and motivation.

Visualizing Success

Visualization is a powerful tool that can help you maintain a positive mindset. Imagine yourself succeeding in various survival tasks, such as finding water, building a sturdy shelter, or making it back to safety. Visualizing these successes not only builds confidence but also prepares your mind to recognize and act on opportunities as they arise. It helps create a mindset where you expect positive outcomes, making you more proactive and resilient when challenges appear.

CONCLUSION

Mental and emotional strength is the cornerstone of successful wilderness survival. By developing techniques for managing isolation and loneliness, building effective coping mechanisms for stress, and cultivating motivation and positivity over time, you strengthen your resilience and increase your chances of thriving in any environment. Combining these psychological skills with practical survival knowledge equips you with the holistic tools necessary to not only survive but also find growth, meaning, and satisfaction in the wilderness.

BOOK 17
SELF-DEFENSE IN THE WILD

Survival in the wilderness isn't just about finding food, water, and shelter. The ability to protect yourself from potential threats—whether they come from wildlife, other humans, or the environment itself—is equally crucial. In remote areas, immediate help is often unavailable, making self-defense skills an essential component of long-term survival. This chapter explores practical approaches to self-defense tailored for wilderness scenarios, focusing on using tools and improvised weapons for protection and learning how to avoid dangerous wildlife encounters. By understanding these strategies, you equip yourself with the skills needed to navigate and thrive in the wild, even when faced with threats.

BASIC SELF-DEFENSE TECHNIQUES FOR WILDERNESS SCENARIOS

In the wilderness, your surroundings can quickly become dangerous if you're unprepared. Self-defense in this context goes beyond conventional combat skills; it's about understanding your environment and using your awareness to anticipate threats before they escalate. Unlike urban self-defense techniques, which often rely on proximity and confined spaces, wilderness self-defense emphasizes maintaining distance, using the landscape to your advantage, and preparing for situations where retreat or avoidance is the best strategy.

Staying Aware of Your Environment

One of the most fundamental skills in wilderness self-defense is situational awareness. The ability to read your surroundings and detect potential hazards—be it wildlife, dangerous terrain, or unknown individuals—can prevent threats from escalating. This heightened state of awareness isn't about being constantly on edge; it's about learning to attune yourself to the subtle changes in your environment. The rustle of leaves, the shift in the wind, or the distant sound of footsteps—these details, often overlooked, can alert you to something approaching long before it arrives.

Practicing this level of awareness means making it a habit to scan your surroundings regularly. As you move through the forest, keep your senses engaged. Observe the patterns in animal behavior; often, they are the first to react to the presence of a predator or another human. If birds suddenly scatter or animals become agitated, take note—this could be a sign that something unusual is happening. By maintaining this connection with your environment, you give yourself the time to respond effectively, whether that means preparing for defense or making a strategic retreat.

Defensive Stance and Movement

In the wilderness, mobility is often your greatest asset. Rather than engaging in a prolonged confrontation, it's more practical to position yourself defensively, with the option to retreat if necessary. A balanced stance, with feet shoulder-width apart and knees slightly bent, allows you to move quickly in any direction. Keeping your hands up and open, you present a non-threatening posture, but you are prepared to block or strike if the need arises.

Should an altercation occur, simple yet effective techniques are invaluable. For instance, using the palm of your hand to strike an assailant's nose or chin provides a powerful response while minimizing the risk of injuring yourself, unlike a punch that might hurt your knuckles. Elbows, too, are valuable tools in close quarters, providing short, sharp strikes to sensitive areas like the ribs or face.

Using Distance and Terrain

Unlike urban environments where walls and structures can limit movement, the wilderness offers a wide range of options for creating distance and using the terrain to your advantage. If you sense a threat approaching, maneuver toward higher ground or position yourself behind natural barriers like rocks or fallen trees. These features not only offer a defensive advantage but also allow you to observe and assess the situation from a secure vantage point.

USING TOOLS AND IMPROVISED WEAPONS FOR PROTECTION

In the wilderness, the tools you carry for survival often double as self-defense weapons. Knowing how to use these tools effectively is a vital skill that can turn the odds in your favor if faced with a threat. The key is understanding the dual purposes of these items and practicing their use not just for survival tasks, but for defense as well.

The Versatility of the Survival Knife

The survival knife is one of the most essential tools in any survivalist's kit. Not only is it indispensable for building shelter, processing food, or carving wood, but it also serves as a powerful means of defense. In the event of an attack, a knife provides a sharp, close-range option for protection. However, wielding it effectively requires confidence and a clear strategy, as its use carries significant risks for both parties involved.

When holding a knife for defense, keep the blade facing outward and maintain a firm grip. Position your body side-on to present a smaller target, and use your free hand to create distance or block if necessary. The objective is not to engage unless there is no other option; the knife should serve as a deterrent, encouraging a would-be attacker to back off. Practicing this posture and movement ensures that if you ever need to use it, you are prepared and confident in its handling.

Improvised Weapons from the Environment

Not all situations allow for the use of a knife, and sometimes, you might find yourself without any conventional weapons at all. In these moments, the wilderness itself becomes a resource. The forest floor is full of potential tools: sturdy branches, sharp stones, and even pine cones can serve as weapons when wielded with skill and precision.

A simple stick, for instance, can be transformed into a spear. Find a long, straight branch and sharpen one end into a point using a rock or knife. To harden it, hold the tip over a flame for a few minutes. This makeshift spear extends your reach, allowing you to fend off animals or attackers from a distance. Similarly, stones are readily available and can be used as projectile weapons or for close-range defense. The act of throwing stones, even if they don't make contact, can create enough distraction or discomfort to give you time to escape.

Creating Defensive Perimeters

Another way to use the environment for defense is by building protective structures around your campsite. Even when you're alone, establishing a defensive perimeter with thorny branches, stacked rocks, or sharpened stakes can deter animals and signal intruders that the area is occupied. This physical barrier serves as both a warning system and an obstacle, giving you time to respond if something approaches during the night.

AVOIDING DANGEROUS WILDLIFE ENCOUNTERS

Encounters with wildlife are inevitable in the wilderness, and while most animals prefer to avoid human contact, some can become aggressive if they feel threatened or surprised. Understanding animal behavior and knowing how to respond appropriately are crucial skills for self-defense in these situations. Rather than engaging directly, the goal is often to de-escalate or avoid the confrontation altogether.

Understanding and Managing Bear Encounters

Bears are among the most formidable animals you might encounter in the wilderness. However, they are typically not aggressive unless they feel threatened or are surprised. The first rule of bear safety is avoidance—making your presence known to prevent an encounter in the first place. While hiking, make noise by clapping, talking loudly, or using a bear bell to alert bears to your presence. This gives them time to move away, reducing the risk of a sudden confrontation.

If you do encounter a bear, the key is to remain calm and assess the situation. Slowly back away while keeping the bear in sight, avoiding direct eye contact, which can be interpreted as a threat. Never turn your back or run, as this can trigger the bear's instinct to chase. If the bear continues to approach, use bear spray if you have it, aiming for its face to create a barrier between you and the animal. In cases where an attack is unavoidable, knowing whether you're dealing with a black bear or a grizzly bear is crucial, as your response should differ. With a black bear, fight back with everything you have, while with a grizzly, playing dead may be your best chance.

Managing Encounters with Mountain Lions

Mountain lions are stealthy and tend to avoid humans, but they can become a threat, especially if they feel cornered or are protecting young. If you spot one, it's essential to remain calm and assertive. Unlike with bears, making yourself appear larger and maintaining eye contact can help deter a mountain lion. Raise your arms, open your jacket, and speak loudly to show that you are not prey.

If the mountain lion continues to approach, pick up a stick or a rock and prepare to defend yourself. Do not crouch or turn your back, as these actions may encourage an attack. Instead, slowly back away while remaining facing the animal. Should an attack occur, fight back aggressively, targeting the face and eyes.

Avoiding Snakes and Other Reptiles

Snakes are another common hazard in many wilderness areas. Most snakes are not aggressive and prefer to flee, but some are venomous and should be treated with caution. Avoid placing your hands or feet where you cannot see clearly, such as in tall grass, under rocks, or inside hollow logs. If you see a snake, give it space to retreat. Do not attempt to handle it or provoke it.

If bitten, remain as calm as possible. Move away from the snake to avoid additional bites, and seek medical help immediately if possible. Immobilize the affected limb to slow the spread of venom and keep it below heart level. Remember, many snake bites are not fatal, but quick action and caution are necessary to ensure the best outcome.

CONCLUSION

Self-defense in the wilderness is as much about preparation and awareness as it is about physical confrontation. By understanding basic defensive techniques, learning how to use tools and improvised weapons, and developing strategies for avoiding dangerous wildlife encounters, you enhance your ability to survive and thrive in the wild. These skills, when combined with a deep respect for the natural environment, allow you to navigate the wilderness with confidence, ensuring that you are prepared for any challenge that may arise.

BOOK 18
GROUP DYNAMICS AND LEADERSHIP

Survival in the wilderness becomes more complex when you are part of a group. While there is strength in numbers, managing a group effectively during a crisis can be a challenge. Leadership plays a crucial role in ensuring that everyone works together, stays safe, and remains motivated under difficult conditions. Whether you find yourself leading a family, friends, or strangers, understanding the dynamics of group behavior and mastering the skills required to build trust and cooperation is essential. This chapter explores how to manage a group during a crisis, develop effective leadership skills tailored for wilderness survival, and foster a sense of unity and trust among group members, ensuring that the group not only survives but thrives.

MANAGING A GROUP DURING A CRISIS

In a survival situation, the presence of a group can be both an advantage and a liability. The group's strength lies in its collective skills, knowledge, and resources; however, the challenge comes from managing different personalities, maintaining morale, and making decisions that benefit everyone. When a crisis hits, the key to managing a group successfully is communication, organization, and adaptability.

Establishing a Clear Chain of Command

In any group, especially during a crisis, uncertainty can lead to confusion and chaos. The first step in managing a group effectively is establishing a clear chain of command. This doesn't mean imposing strict authority; instead, it's about creating a structure where decisions can be made efficiently and communicated clearly. Designating a leader or leadership team early on helps prevent power struggles and gives the group a sense of direction and stability. When everyone understands who is responsible for making key decisions, it reduces anxiety and allows the group to focus on survival tasks rather than on disagreements or confusion.

The leader should also recognize the importance of delegation. Rather than attempting to manage every aspect of the group's survival, delegating responsibilities according to individuals' skills and strengths fosters a sense of ownership and accountability among group members. For instance, one person may be skilled in navigation and take charge of planning routes, while another may be adept at building shelter. By giving each member a role that suits their abilities, you empower them to contribute meaningfully and feel valued.

Setting Common Goals and Priorities

In a survival situation, setting common goals is vital for unifying the group. A crisis can cause panic, and people may begin to focus solely on their individual needs. It's the leader's job to bring the group together by emphasizing shared objectives, such as finding water, securing shelter, or locating food sources. This not only aligns the group's efforts but also gives members a sense of purpose and a clear focus, reducing the chances of discord.

It's crucial to communicate these goals clearly and ensure that everyone understands why each task is important. For example, if the priority is building a shelter before nightfall, explain the risks of exposure and how working together to construct a solid shelter benefits everyone. By framing objectives in terms of collective benefit, you foster a spirit of cooperation and solidarity. It's also helpful to establish shorter-term milestones that build towards long-term goals. Achieving these milestones keeps morale high and gives the group a sense of accomplishment and progress.

Managing Conflicts and Disputes

Disagreements are inevitable when people are under stress, especially in a high-stakes survival scenario. Part of managing a group effectively is anticipating and resolving conflicts before they escalate. The best approach is to listen actively and mediate disputes with fairness and empathy. In the wilderness, holding grudges or allowing tensions to fester can be dangerous, as they undermine group cohesion and can lead to a breakdown in communication and cooperation.

When conflicts arise, encourage open dialogue and ensure that everyone has a chance to voice their concerns. Create a space where people feel heard, but also remind them of the larger context: survival. When individuals see that their grievances are being taken seriously, they are more likely to move past conflicts and focus on the shared mission. The leader should act as a neutral party, helping to find compromises or resolutions that keep the group united. However, in situations where consensus cannot be reached, the leader must be prepared to make the final decision and ensure that it is communicated clearly, keeping the group's goals and safety as the top priority.

EFFECTIVE LEADERSHIP SKILLS FOR WILDERNESS SURVIVAL

In the wilderness, leadership extends beyond making decisions; it involves inspiring and motivating others, maintaining morale, and ensuring the group's physical and emotional needs are met. An effective leader in a survival scenario must adapt their approach to the unique challenges of the environment while leveraging their own strengths and those of the group.

Leading by Example

The most powerful form of leadership is leading by example. In a survival situation, words alone may not be enough to inspire confidence or motivate action; demonstrating resilience, resourcefulness, and commitment through your actions is far more impactful. For instance, if the group needs to build a shelter, take the initiative by gathering materials and showing others how to construct it. When group members see the leader engaging actively and working alongside them, it builds trust and encourages them to contribute their own efforts.

This type of leadership also involves showing vulnerability and honesty when necessary. Admitting that you don't have all the answers but are committed to finding solutions together can create a sense of camaraderie and trust. It's about being transparent, especially when conditions are difficult. Sharing the burden of uncertainty with the group, rather than pretending to have everything under control, can foster solidarity.

Decision-Making Under Pressure

In a wilderness survival scenario, decisions often need to be made quickly and under pressure. An effective leader must balance decisiveness with caution, assessing risks and weighing options before acting. This requires a calm and focused mindset, especially in moments of crisis. The ability to stay composed and think clearly under stress reassures the group and prevents panic from spreading.

When making decisions, it's beneficial to involve the group in the process when possible. Seeking input from members not only helps gather diverse perspectives but also makes individuals feel valued and included. This collaborative approach can strengthen the group's commitment to the plan and reduce resistance to decisions that may be difficult or unpopular. For example, if the group needs to decide whether to move camp due to approaching bad weather, consult those with expertise in navigation or understanding local terrain. Even if the leader makes the final call, the process of involving others can help build consensus and trust.

Maintaining Morale and Motivation

Keeping spirits high is one of the greatest challenges in a survival scenario, especially as time wears on and the initial adrenaline fades. The leader must be attuned to the emotional state of the group, recognizing signs of fatigue, fear, or despair. This requires a compassionate approach—acknowledging the difficulties everyone faces while finding ways to boost morale.

Celebrating small victories, such as finding a new food source or completing a shelter, can be a powerful motivator. Recognizing the contributions of individual members reinforces the value of each person's efforts, helping to sustain a positive group dynamic. Additionally, organizing group activities that break the monotony—like storytelling, games, or small physical exercises—can provide a psychological boost and remind everyone of their shared humanity.

The leader must also maintain optimism, even when faced with setbacks. This doesn't mean ignoring the reality of challenges but rather focusing on the group's strengths and the progress made so far. Expressing confidence in the group's ability to overcome obstacles can inspire others to persevere and stay motivated.

BUILDING TRUST AND COOPERATION AMONG GROUP MEMBERS

Trust is the foundation of any effective group dynamic, particularly in a survival scenario where everyone's safety depends on cooperation and collaboration. Building trust involves establishing open communication, encouraging collaboration, and fostering a sense of mutual reliance. When people trust one another, they are more likely to work together effectively, share resources willingly, and support each other through difficult times.

Fostering Open Communication

Clear and open communication is crucial for building trust within the group. The leader must create an environment where members feel comfortable voicing their opinions, concerns, and suggestions. This requires not only speaking clearly and with purpose but also listening actively. Demonstrating that you value each person's input encourages openness and transparency.

Regular group check-ins are an effective way to maintain this communication. Setting aside time each day for the group to come together, discuss the day's progress, and address any issues allows for continuous feedback and adjustment of plans. These meetings also provide an opportunity for group members to express any concerns they might have in a safe and supportive environment. By making communication a priority, you reinforce the sense that everyone's voice matters and that decisions are made collectively for the benefit of all.

Encouraging Collaboration and Shared Responsibility

In a survival scenario, no one can do everything alone; fostering collaboration is essential. The leader's role is to identify the skills and strengths of each member and encourage them to share their knowledge with the group. For example, if one member has experience with tracking or plant identification, they can teach others, turning their expertise into a group asset. This not only builds confidence in the individual but also empowers the entire group with new skills.

Shared responsibility also means ensuring that everyone has a role. When each member knows they have an important function—whether it's gathering firewood, keeping watch, or cooking—it strengthens their commitment to the group's success. Rotating tasks and roles can also help prevent burnout and promote a sense of fairness, ensuring that no one person feels overburdened.

Promoting Mutual Support and Unity

Mutual support is the heart of effective group dynamics. In the wilderness, individuals may face physical exhaustion, emotional stress, or moments of fear. Encouraging a culture where members support one another in these times is vital. This can mean offering assistance when someone struggles with a task, sharing resources equally, or simply listening when someone needs to express their frustrations.

The leader must set the example for this culture of support. Demonstrating empathy, being willing to help others without hesitation, and showing respect for each member's efforts foster a sense of unity. When group members feel that they are not alone and that others genuinely care about their well-being, it strengthens their resolve and commitment to the group's collective success.

Dealing with Group Fatigue and Setbacks

Long-term survival inevitably involves setbacks—bad weather, injuries, or failures to find food can impact group morale. The key to maintaining unity and trust during these difficult times is to address challenges openly and without placing blame. Framing setbacks as opportunities to learn and adapt can shift the group's perspective from frustration to resilience.

The leader should also be mindful of group fatigue. Long days and physical hardship take a toll, and it's important to allow time for rest and recovery. Ensuring that everyone gets adequate sleep, hydration, and nutrition is a fundamental part of leadership. Recognizing when the group needs a break, even if it means delaying certain tasks, shows that the leader values the well-being of the group over immediate productivity. This balance between progress and rest is crucial for maintaining long-term group cohesion.

CONCLUSION

Leading a group in a wilderness survival scenario requires a combination of strategic decision-making, empathy, and adaptability. By managing group dynamics effectively, fostering collaboration, and building trust, a leader can turn a group of individuals into a cohesive, resilient unit. These skills not only increase the group's chances of survival but also ensure that each member feels valued, heard, and supported. In the end, effective leadership transforms the wilderness from a place of potential danger into an opportunity for unity, growth, and shared achievement.

BOOK 19

FAMILY SURVIVAL TECHNIQUES

Surviving in the wilderness alone is challenging enough, but when you're with family—particularly with children—it becomes a complex undertaking that requires careful planning, cooperation, and adaptability. Ensuring the safety, well-being, and participation of all family members is vital for long-term survival, as is creating an environment where everyone has a role and feels engaged. This chapter explores techniques for ensuring children's safety and participation, creating specific roles and responsibilities for family members, and building collaborative shelters that accommodate the needs of an entire family unit. By mastering these family-oriented survival skills, you can transform the wilderness from a place of danger into a haven where everyone contributes to the group's success and well-being.

ENSURING CHILDREN'S SAFETY AND PARTICIPATION

When surviving with children, their safety becomes the highest priority. Children bring both unique challenges and strengths to a survival situation. They may lack the physical strength or experience of adults, but they often possess adaptability, enthusiasm, and curiosity that can be harnessed positively. Ensuring their safety requires vigilance, but also a proactive approach that involves them in the survival process, helping them learn and contribute in meaningful ways.

Establishing Safe Boundaries and Rules

The first step in ensuring children's safety in the wilderness is to establish clear boundaries and rules. It's important to create a sense of structure that children can understand and follow, even in an unpredictable environment. For instance, setting a rule that they must always stay within sight of an adult reduces the risk of them wandering off. Teach them to recognize key landmarks, such as large trees, distinctive rock formations, or the sound of running water, so they know how to find their way back if they become separated from the group.

Children should also be taught basic emergency procedures, such as what to do if they get lost. A simple yet effective rule is to stay in one place and make noise (like shouting or whistling) so they can be located quickly. Equipping them with a whistle or another noise-making device ensures they have a way to signal for help. While the wilderness can be an unpredictable place, providing these basic survival strategies gives children a sense of security and autonomy, reducing their fear and increasing their preparedness.

Involving Children in Survival Tasks

Involving children in survival tasks not only keeps them occupied but also teaches them valuable skills that contribute to their safety and the family's overall success. While their physical abilities might limit them from more demanding tasks, they can still participate in simpler activities like gathering small firewood, picking berries, or collecting water. These tasks are not only manageable for children but also provide them with a sense of purpose and responsibility.

Moreover, including children in these activities helps them feel like valued members of the group, boosting their morale and confidence. Even something as simple as helping to prepare meals or sort supplies can be framed as an important contribution, showing them that they play a crucial role in the family's survival. By teaching children these skills early, you also prepare them to take on more significant responsibilities as they grow and adapt to the wilderness environment.

Educating Children About Nature's Dangers

Education is one of the most effective ways to keep children safe in the wilderness. Teaching them to recognize potential hazards—such as poisonous plants, dangerous animals, or unstable terrain—empowers them to make safer choices. Start with simple lessons that match their age and comprehension level. For example, teach them that bright-colored berries and mushrooms are often signs of toxicity, or show them how to identify animal tracks that could indicate predators in the area.

Another crucial lesson is to instill a respect for nature without creating unnecessary fear. Children should understand that animals, while often harmless, can become dangerous if approached or provoked. Encourage them to observe wildlife from a distance and explain how to interpret animal behavior, such as the warning signs of an aggressive bear or the presence of snakes. Equipping them with this knowledge helps children navigate the wilderness safely and responsibly.

CREATING ROLES AND RESPONSIBILITIES FOR FAMILY MEMBERS

Surviving as a family requires an organized approach where everyone knows their roles and responsibilities. By assigning tasks based on each family member's strengths, skills, and capabilities, you create a sense of structure and purpose that keeps everyone engaged and working toward common goals. This approach not only maximizes efficiency but also enhances the group's morale by ensuring that everyone feels valued.

Assessing Skills and Assigning Roles

The first step in creating effective roles for each family member is to assess their skills and strengths. Adults may have specialized knowledge—such as first aid, navigation, or fire-building—that naturally position them for leadership roles. However, it's equally important to recognize the abilities of younger family members. Teenagers, for instance, may have the physical capability and enthusiasm for gathering resources, helping with shelter construction, or assisting in hunting or fishing.

Once you've assessed the skills within the group, assign specific roles that align with these abilities. For example, an adult with medical knowledge could be designated as the group's medic, while another who is proficient in navigation could take on the role of scout, responsible for mapping out safe routes and identifying resources. Teenagers could assist in physical tasks, such as gathering firewood or building shelters, while younger children can participate in simpler but essential jobs like sorting supplies, maintaining water stores, or keeping the camp tidy.

Rotating Responsibilities to Prevent Fatigue

To prevent burnout and ensure that skills are distributed evenly among all family members, it's important to rotate responsibilities periodically. This not only keeps everyone engaged but also ensures that each person learns multiple survival skills, enhancing the group's overall resilience. For example, if one person is responsible for cooking meals each day, rotate this task among other capable family members so that everyone becomes familiar with foraging, cooking over an open fire, and preparing food safely.

Rotating tasks also prevents any one person from feeling overwhelmed by their responsibilities. In a survival situation, maintaining energy and motivation is crucial, and sharing the workload helps sustain the group's strength. By encouraging flexibility in roles, you also prepare each family member to step into another's responsibilities if necessary, creating a more adaptable and unified group dynamic.

Balancing Leadership and Collaboration

While it's essential to have a clear leadership structure, it's equally important to foster a sense of collaboration within the family. An effective leader doesn't simply delegate tasks; they involve others in decision-making processes and seek input from all members. For example, when deciding where to set up camp, discuss the options with the family, considering factors like proximity to water, visibility, and natural protection from the elements. This collaborative approach ensures that everyone feels their opinions are valued, which strengthens family bonds and builds trust.

Balancing leadership with collaboration also allows for the development of younger family members into leadership roles. By involving them in planning and decision-making, they gain confidence and learn the skills needed to lead in the future. This approach not only empowers individuals but also strengthens the family as a whole, ensuring that leadership is not dependent on one person alone.

BUILDING COLLABORATIVE SHELTERS FOR FAMILIES

When building shelter for a family in the wilderness, it's important to think beyond individual needs and create a space that offers security, comfort, and enough room for everyone to stay together. Building collaborative shelters not only provides physical protection but also fosters a sense of unity and cooperation, as everyone plays a part in constructing and maintaining the shared living space.

Choosing the Right Location for a Family Shelter

The location of a family shelter is critical. It must be situated in an area that offers protection from the elements, access to resources, and safety from wildlife. Look for sites that are elevated enough to avoid flooding but still close enough to water sources for easy access. Natural windbreaks, such as cliffs, dense trees, or large boulders, can offer protection from harsh winds and help regulate temperature.

It's essential to ensure that the shelter site is clear of potential hazards, like loose rocks that could fall or areas where wildlife may frequent. Involve the family in scouting and evaluating potential sites, teaching them what to look for and how to assess the safety of a location. This involvement not only ensures that the best site is chosen but also educates everyone on what makes a good shelter location, which is a valuable skill for future survival scenarios.

Designing and Building Collaborative Shelters

When constructing a shelter for a family, the design should accommodate multiple people comfortably. A simple lean-to or debris hut might be sufficient for one person, but for a family, you need a structure that provides space for sleeping, storage, and protection from the elements. Consider building a long-term family shelter, such as a frame structure made from sturdy branches and reinforced with natural materials like leaves, moss, and grass for insulation.

Involve all family members in the construction process. Assign tasks based on each person's ability: younger children can gather smaller branches and leaves, while older children and adults work on the main framework and insulation. By working together, you not only build the shelter faster but also create a collaborative environment where everyone feels responsible for its maintenance and upkeep.

If the group plans to stay in one location for an extended period, consider building a more substantial log cabin-style shelter using fallen trees or large branches. This type of shelter offers more durability and insulation, making it suitable for colder climates. Building such a structure is labor-intensive but can be turned into a family project, where each member plays a specific role in collecting materials, constructing walls, or insulating the roof.

Ensuring Comfort and Safety Within the Shelter

Once the shelter is built, ensuring it remains comfortable and safe for all family members is a continuous task. Establish a designated area for sleeping that is elevated off the ground to reduce exposure to cold and insects. Use natural materials, such as pine needles or dry leaves, as bedding for insulation and comfort. Assign roles for maintaining the shelter, such as reinforcing the roof before rain or keeping the area clean to deter wildlife.

Additionally, create a central area for cooking and warmth, ensuring that it's ventilated properly to avoid smoke buildup while still retaining heat. This area can become a focal point for the family, where meals are prepared, and stories are shared, fostering a sense of community and morale. Teaching children how to safely manage the fire and cook simple meals also contributes to their sense of involvement and helps them develop essential survival skills.

Building Additional Functional Areas

For a larger family unit, it may be beneficial to build additional functional areas around the main shelter. A storage area for food, firewood, and tools helps keep the living space organized and ensures essential resources are protected from the elements. Consider building raised platforms or lean-tos specifically for storage, keeping supplies dry and secure.

If the environment allows, construct a latrine at a safe distance from the shelter to maintain hygiene and minimize contamination risks. Building these additional functional spaces reinforces the idea of a collaborative survival effort and shows children the importance of maintaining a structured and organized living environment in the wilderness.

ADAPTING AND IMPROVING SHELTER OVER TIME

The shelter should not remain static; as the family adjusts to their environment, they can continue to improve and adapt the structure to suit changing needs. Over time, you may choose to add more insulation for colder weather, expand the shelter to accommodate more space, or build protective barriers around the perimeter to keep out animals. These modifications not only enhance safety and comfort but also keep the group engaged in a shared project that benefits everyone.

By encouraging family members to propose improvements and work together on enhancements, you foster a sense of ownership and responsibility that extends beyond basic survival. Children, in particular, can be given creative freedom to suggest ways to make the shelter more comfortable or efficient, teaching them problem-solving skills and encouraging them to think innovatively about their environment.

CONCLUSION

Family survival in the wilderness demands a unique set of skills and strategies that go beyond individual survival. Ensuring the safety and participation of children, creating roles and responsibilities tailored to each family member's abilities, and building collaborative shelters are all crucial components for success. By focusing on collaboration, education, and structured involvement, families not only increase their chances of survival but also strengthen their bonds and resilience in the face of challenges. In the wilderness, a unified family becomes a powerful force, capable of turning the environment into a place of safety, learning, and growth.

BOOK 20
PREPARING FOR WILDFIRES

Wildfires are one of the most dangerous and unpredictable threats you may encounter in the wilderness. They can move rapidly, fueled by wind and dry vegetation, and often leave little time for escape. Preparing for wildfires involves more than just knowing how to respond in the moment; it requires a comprehensive approach that includes planning evacuation routes, building fire-resistant shelters, and monitoring conditions that may indicate a wildfire threat. In this chapter, we explore how to create a fire evacuation plan, build shelters that minimize the risk of fire damage, and effectively monitor and respond to wildfire threats. By understanding these strategies, you can significantly increase your chances of survival in areas prone to wildfires.

CREATING A FIRE EVACUATION PLAN

A well-thought-out fire evacuation plan is crucial for survival in wildfire-prone areas. Wildfires can spread quickly, often leaving little time to react, so having a clear plan that everyone understands can mean the difference between life and death. The goal of a fire evacuation plan is to identify safe routes, establish evacuation protocols, and ensure that all necessary equipment and supplies are ready at a moment's notice.

Identifying Safe Evacuation Routes

The first step in developing an effective evacuation plan is identifying safe routes. This involves understanding the topography of the area and mapping out multiple escape paths. Ideally, these routes should lead to open areas or bodies of water, where fire cannot spread easily. Avoid routes that pass through dense forests or dry grasslands, as these areas are likely to burn quickly and may become blocked.

When choosing routes, consider the direction of the prevailing winds, as wildfires often move with the wind. Map out paths that move away from the wind's direction and lead to safety. If possible, familiarize yourself with local firebreaks—gaps in vegetation that are intentionally cleared to slow the spread of fire—and incorporate these into your plan. Natural firebreaks like rivers, streams, and rocky outcrops can also provide safe havens and routes of escape.

It's essential to have multiple routes planned in case your primary path is compromised. Mark these routes clearly on a physical map and memorize them, ensuring you have alternatives no matter which direction the fire approaches. Practice these evacuation routes with everyone in your group or family, so they become second nature if an emergency arises.

Establishing a Communication Protocol

In a wildfire situation, communication is critical. Establishing a clear communication protocol ensures that all members of your group stay informed and know how to react quickly. If you're in a family or group setting, designate a point of contact—a person responsible for monitoring conditions and making the decision to evacuate. This person should have access to a radio, if available, or any other reliable communication device to stay updated on fire developments.

Additionally, agree on emergency signals that everyone understands, such as whistle blasts or hand signals, in case you lose visual or verbal contact. These signals can indicate when it's time to regroup, start evacuating, or communicate other crucial information. Practicing these signals ahead of time ensures that they are clear and effective in the midst of a crisis.

Packing a "Go-Bag"

A go-bag is an essential part of your fire evacuation plan. This bag should be packed and ready at all times, containing the supplies necessary for a quick evacuation. Key items include:

- First aid kit: For treating burns, cuts, and other injuries.
- Water and purification tablets: To stay hydrated if you have to move quickly.
- Protective clothing: Long-sleeve shirts, pants, sturdy boots, and a face covering (such as an N95 mask) to protect against smoke and heat.
- Emergency shelter: A lightweight, heat-resistant emergency blanket or bivouac sack that can offer temporary protection if caught in a dangerous situation.
- Fireproof bag: For important documents, such as maps, communication devices, and identification.

By having this bag prepared and accessible, you ensure that you are ready to leave at a moment's notice, maximizing your chances of escaping safely.

BUILDING FIRE-RESISTANT SHELTERS

Even with a solid evacuation plan, there may be times when fleeing is not possible, and you must rely on your shelter for protection. Building a fire-resistant shelter in the wilderness is a proactive way to reduce the risk of injury during a wildfire. While no shelter is entirely fireproof, careful planning and construction can significantly minimize the dangers.

Choosing the Right Location for a Shelter

The location of your shelter is the first line of defense against wildfires. Avoid building shelters in areas with dense vegetation, dry grass, or near trees with low-hanging branches, as these can ignite easily and spread fire rapidly. Instead, look for clearings or areas with sparse vegetation. Rocky terrains, open fields, or areas near large bodies of water are ideal, as they provide natural buffers against fire.

Position your shelter on level ground or on the windward side of a hill, where wind currents are less likely to carry flames directly toward it. Avoid building in valleys or depressions where smoke and heat may accumulate, creating a more dangerous environment.

Constructing the Shelter with Fire-Resistant Materials

When building a shelter, choosing the right materials is essential for fire resistance. Natural stone, clay, and sand can all be used to build or reinforce the structure's walls and roof. If possible, incorporate these materials to create a thermal barrier that slows down the spread of fire and protects against intense heat.

For the roof, opt for materials like green, leafy branches with high moisture content, which are less likely to ignite. Avoid using dry wood or leaves, as these are highly flammable. If you have access to clay or mud, applying a layer over the roof and walls can provide additional insulation and fire resistance. The mud acts as a barrier, reducing the risk of flames penetrating the shelter.

Clearing a Safety Zone Around the Shelter

An essential step in building a fire-resistant shelter is creating a defensible space around it. This involves clearing vegetation, debris, and any combustible materials within a radius of at least 30 feet (9 meters) around your shelter. This zone acts as a buffer, preventing fire from reaching the structure quickly. Remove dry leaves, twigs, and brush, and trim any low-hanging branches that could ignite.

If possible, dig a shallow trench around the perimeter of your shelter. This trench can help slow the advance of flames and act as a break that prevents fire from spreading directly to your shelter. Additionally, keeping a supply of water nearby—whether from a stream, pond, or water containers—provides a resource for dousing small fires that may start near the shelter.

Creating an Emergency Fire Shelter

An emergency fire shelter is a last-resort option if you cannot evacuate or your primary shelter becomes compromised. This temporary refuge can be made using heat-resistant materials like reflective foil blankets or bivouac sacks designed for fire protection. If you do not have access to these, constructing a fire trench can offer temporary protection.

To create a fire trench, dig a narrow trench deep enough for you to lie flat in. Cover yourself with dirt or sand, leaving a small air pocket for breathing. This method is not ideal, but it can reduce exposure to flames and radiant heat, giving you a better chance of survival if a wildfire passes over your location.

MONITORING AND RESPONDING TO WILDFIRE THREATS

Staying aware of wildfire threats and responding proactively is essential for survival. Understanding the signs of a potential wildfire, monitoring weather conditions, and knowing how to react quickly are all critical skills in a fire-prone wilderness environment.

Recognizing Early Signs of a Wildfire

Wildfires often provide warning signs before they become immediate threats. The most obvious indicator is the smell of smoke or the sight of a distant haze. If you detect smoke, assess its color and intensity. Thick, black smoke often indicates a nearby, fast-moving fire, while lighter, white smoke may suggest a less intense burn or one farther away.

The direction of the wind is another important factor. If the wind is blowing smoke directly toward your location, the fire may be moving in your direction. Watch for falling ash or embers carried by the wind—these are signs that the fire is approaching, and embers can ignite new fires ahead of the main blaze.

If you have access to a radio, keep it tuned to local emergency broadcasts for updates on fire conditions. In the absence of technology, rely on your senses and environmental cues, such as observing how wildlife behaves. Animals often sense danger before humans and may flee the area in large numbers when a fire is nearby. Such behavior can serve as a natural alert system, prompting you to take precautions.

Monitoring Weather Conditions and Fire Risks

Understanding the weather patterns in your environment is crucial for predicting wildfire risks. Hot, dry conditions combined with strong winds are the perfect recipe for a wildfire. Before settling in an area, observe the prevailing weather patterns and the direction of the winds. If a windstorm is approaching, prepare to evacuate or reinforce your shelter, as fires spread rapidly under windy conditions.

Additionally, keep an eye on the state of the vegetation around you. If the area is dry, with brittle grasses and fallen leaves, the risk of fire increases significantly. It's important to stay proactive—if you notice these signs, clear the area around your shelter and have your go-bag ready, anticipating that evacuation may become necessary.

Responding to Fire Threats

When a wildfire threatens your location, decisive and quick action is vital. The first step is to assess the direction of the fire and its proximity. If the fire is approaching rapidly, evacuate immediately along one of the pre-planned routes, moving toward a natural firebreak or a body of water. Remember that smoke can obscure visibility, so stay low to the ground to avoid inhaling toxic fumes, and use landmarks or pre-marked routes to guide your path.

If evacuation is not possible and the fire is close, retreat to your fire-resistant shelter. Close off any openings and keep the area around the shelter as clear as possible. Wet down the walls and roof if you have access to water, as this can provide temporary protection against encroaching flames. As a last resort, use your emergency fire shelter or fire trench to reduce exposure.

If you manage to reach an open area, such as a clearing or a riverbank, position yourself with your back to the wind and the fire, staying close to the ground. Cover your mouth and nose with a damp cloth to reduce smoke inhalation, and be prepared to move if the fire changes direction.

RECOVERING AND REBUILDING AFTER A WILDFIRE

Surviving a wildfire is only the first step; the aftermath can present its own set of challenges. Returning to a burnt area requires caution, as falling trees, weakened structures, and lingering embers can still pose risks. Before returning to your shelter or camp, assess the damage carefully, ensuring the area is stable and no immediate hazards remain.

Rebuilding after a wildfire starts with clearing the debris and ash around your shelter site. If your shelter was damaged, prioritize building a temporary structure before reconstructing a long-term one. Use non-burnt materials, like green wood or stone, to create a base that is less likely to ignite if another fire occurs.

Additionally, monitor the environment for signs of regrowth. Wildfires often open the land to new growth, which may provide fresh resources like edible plants or new game trails. Adapting to these changes and using them to your advantage helps you recover and thrive in the altered landscape.

CONCLUSION

Wildfires are a formidable threat in the wilderness, but with preparation, awareness, and the right strategies, they are survivable. By creating a fire evacuation plan, building fire-resistant shelters, and knowing how to monitor and respond to wildfire threats, you increase your chances of escaping unharmed and protecting your resources. This knowledge empowers you to not only survive the immediate danger but also rebuild and adapt to life in the aftermath of a wildfire, transforming the wilderness into a place of resilience and safety rather than fear.

BOOK 21
EARTHQUAKE READINESS

Earthquakes are sudden, unpredictable, and potentially devastating natural events that can strike without warning. Whether you are in a city or the wilderness, understanding how to prepare for, survive, and respond to earthquakes is crucial for ensuring your safety and the safety of those around you. This chapter explores essential safety precautions to take before, during, and after earthquakes, strategies for reinforcing shelters against earthquake damage, and the importance of creating effective evacuation and communication plans. By mastering these techniques, you can build a resilient approach to earthquake survival, enhancing your ability to protect yourself and your loved ones in a crisis.

SAFETY PRECAUTIONS BEFORE, DURING, AND AFTER EARTHQUAKES

Earthquakes can cause a wide range of hazards, including falling debris, landslides, and fires. To minimize the risk of injury or damage, it's important to implement safety measures before an earthquake occurs, understand what actions to take during the shaking, and have a clear plan for the aftermath.

Before an Earthquake: Preparation and Planning

The best way to survive an earthquake is through proactive preparation. Begin by assessing your environment, whether you are in a city, at home, or in a wilderness shelter. Identify potential hazards that could become dangerous during an earthquake, such as heavy objects that could fall, unsecured furniture, or loose rocks and debris if you're outdoors. Secure or remove these hazards to reduce the risk of injury.

If you are in a built structure, make sure to reinforce furniture and appliances by anchoring them to walls or floors. Items like bookshelves, cabinets, and heavy equipment should be fixed to avoid tipping over during seismic activity. Ensure that your emergency supplies, such as first aid kits, water, and non-perishable food, are stored in accessible, secure locations.

Additionally, familiarize yourself with the geography of the area. Know where fault lines, cliffs, and unstable terrain are located, as these can influence how the earthquake impacts the environment. If you're in a city, locate safe spots such as door frames or sturdy furniture under which you can take cover. In the wilderness, identify open areas away from trees, cliffs, or loose rock formations that could pose a risk.

Creating an Emergency Plan

Every family or group should have an earthquake emergency plan. This plan should include designated safe spots for taking cover, evacuation routes, and a system for regrouping if separated. Practice earthquake drills regularly so that everyone knows what to do when the shaking starts. Drills should include where to take cover, how to protect yourself from falling debris, and the quickest routes to reach safety.

Prepare an emergency kit that includes essential items such as:

- Water and purification tablets
- First aid kit with supplies for treating injuries
- Non-perishable food for several days
- Protective gear, such as sturdy shoes and gloves
- Communication tools, such as a battery-powered or hand-crank radio to receive updates

Having this kit ready ensures you are prepared to survive both the immediate impact and the aftermath, when resources may be limited.

During an Earthquake: Immediate Actions

When an earthquake strikes, your immediate response is crucial. The key is to drop, cover, and hold on. If you are indoors, drop to your hands and knees to prevent being knocked over. Take cover under sturdy furniture like a table or desk, or protect your head and neck with your arms if no shelter is available. Hold on to the furniture until the shaking stops to maintain cover, as the earthquake may move objects around.

If you are outdoors, move away from buildings, trees, power lines, and anything that could fall. Find an open space and stay low, protecting your head and neck. Avoid cliffs, steep slopes, or any areas where landslides could occur.

In the wilderness, the primary goal is to move to an open area. Avoid camping under trees, near cliffs, or in areas where loose rocks could become hazardous. When the shaking begins, drop to the ground and cover your head until the tremors stop. If you are near water, be aware of the risk of tsunamis if you are in a coastal region. Move to higher ground immediately after the shaking ceases if you are close to a coastline.

After an Earthquake: Assessing and Responding

The aftermath of an earthquake can be as dangerous as the event itself. After the initial shaking, be prepared for aftershocks, which are smaller tremors that can occur minutes, hours, or even days later. These can be almost as strong as the main quake and cause further damage to already weakened structures.

Once the shaking stops, carefully assess your surroundings for immediate hazards. If you are indoors, check for signs of structural damage such as cracks in walls, leaning beams, or broken glass. If the building appears unstable, evacuate as quickly and safely as possible.

If you're in the wilderness, be cautious of landslides, falling trees, or rocks that may have been loosened during the earthquake. Avoid cliffs and steep slopes, and move to stable ground if your current location shows signs of instability.

Check on the safety of others in your group and administer first aid where necessary. Be cautious when using open flames, as gas lines may have ruptured, leading to the risk of fires. If you smell gas or suspect a leak, move away from the area and avoid using lighters or electrical equipment.

REINFORCING SHELTERS AGAINST EARTHQUAKE DAMAGE

Building or reinforcing a shelter to withstand earthquakes requires careful consideration of materials, design, and location. Whether constructing a temporary wilderness shelter or retrofitting an existing structure, the goal is to create a space that can protect you during seismic activity and provide a safe haven afterward.

Choosing an Earthquake-Resistant Shelter Location

Location is critical when it comes to building a shelter that can withstand earthquakes. In the wilderness, avoid building on slopes, near cliffs, or in areas with loose rock formations, as these locations are prone to landslides and falling debris during an earthquake. Instead, choose a site that is on stable, flat ground, ideally in an open area away from large trees or boulders that could become hazards.

If you are in an urban or suburban environment, assess the safety of your current location. Avoid structures that are old, poorly maintained, or constructed from materials that do not withstand seismic activity well, such as unreinforced brick. If possible, retrofit your shelter by reinforcing walls with steel bracing or installing seismic straps for heavy items like water heaters.

Constructing a Flexible Shelter Design

Flexibility is key to earthquake-resistant structures. Rigid shelters are more likely to suffer damage during seismic activity, as they cannot absorb and distribute the energy generated by the ground shaking. When building a wilderness shelter, use natural materials such as logs or bamboo, which have some give and can flex under stress. Reinforce the structure with rope or vine bindings that allow movement but prevent collapse.

If you're building a more permanent shelter, consider a frame structure made from wood rather than stone or brick. Wood frames are lighter and more flexible, making them less likely to collapse during an earthquake. For added stability, cross-brace the walls and use triangular supports, which are structurally strong and distribute force more evenly.

Securing and Anchoring the Shelter

Properly anchoring your shelter is essential to prevent it from shifting during an earthquake. In the wilderness, dig post holes deep enough to secure the frame of the shelter, using rocks or dirt to reinforce the base. If available, use ropes or straps to tie down the structure and secure it to stable trees or large boulders nearby.

In an existing structure, secure heavy furniture and appliances to walls using brackets or straps. Install latches on cabinets to prevent items from falling out, and ensure that hanging objects like light fixtures are fastened securely. By reinforcing the interior of your shelter, you minimize the risk of injury from falling debris during an earthquake.

EVACUATION AND COMMUNICATION PLANS FOR EARTHQUAKES

When an earthquake occurs, having a well-established evacuation and communication plan can make a significant difference in your ability to respond quickly and safely. Earthquakes can disrupt communication networks, making it essential to have a strategy that does not rely solely on technology. By planning ahead and practicing these procedures, you ensure that you and your group can act effectively during an emergency.

Developing an Evacuation Plan

An evacuation plan should be tailored to your environment, whether it's a wilderness shelter, a suburban home, or an urban apartment. The plan must include multiple evacuation routes, as the primary route may be blocked or unsafe due to debris or structural damage. If you are in a building, identify safe exits and alternate stairwells. Avoid using elevators, as power outages or damage could trap you inside.

In the wilderness, map out routes that lead to open areas away from cliffs or loose rock formations. Make sure everyone in your group knows these routes and has practiced them during drills. It's also important to establish regrouping points—locations where you will meet if you become separated during the evacuation.

Establishing Communication Protocols

Communication is essential during and after an earthquake, but traditional means of communication, like cell phones, may not work if towers are damaged. Prepare by equipping your group with two-way radios or walkie-talkies that do not rely on cell networks. Radios that run on batteries or are solar-powered are ideal for maintaining contact during emergencies.

Agree on emergency signals for when verbal communication isn't possible. Whistles, flashlight signals, or other sound-based methods can alert group members of danger or signal the need to regroup. Ensure that everyone understands these signals and knows how to use them.

In addition, establish a communication tree with a trusted contact outside the earthquake-prone area. This person can act as a relay point for updates and instructions if local communication systems are down. Practice reporting in with this contact during drills, ensuring that your emergency plans remain consistent and reliable.

Organizing Emergency Supplies for Evacuation

An essential component of any evacuation plan is preparing and organizing emergency supplies. The go-bag, as described earlier, is crucial, but for earthquake-specific readiness, include additional items like:

- Dust masks: Protect against debris and dust if buildings collapse.
- Goggles: Protect your eyes from debris and smoke.
- Sturdy gloves: Useful for clearing debris and protecting hands during evacuation.
- Extra batteries: For radios, flashlights, and other communication tools.

Organize these supplies so they are easy to grab and carry during an evacuation. Place them near exit points and make sure every group member knows their location.

RESPONDING AND RECOVERING AFTER AN EARTHQUAKE

Once the shaking stops, the immediate task is to assess your surroundings and regroup with your team or family members. Look for signs of damage, such as cracks in the ground, fallen trees, or landslides, and avoid these areas. Move cautiously, as aftershocks may occur, further destabilizing the terrain.

After ensuring everyone's safety, begin assessing the condition of your shelter and supplies. If your shelter is damaged, seek out open areas that remain safe, avoiding areas near cliffs or unstable slopes. If you have communication tools like radios, tune in for emergency broadcasts and updates from local authorities.

If you are in an urban or suburban area, follow local guidelines for evacuations, as emergency services will likely be overwhelmed. In the wilderness, rely on your prepared routes and regrouping points to navigate safely.

CONCLUSION

Earthquake readiness requires a proactive approach that combines preparation, awareness, and strategic response. By understanding the safety precautions to take before, during, and after earthquakes, reinforcing shelters against damage, and developing effective evacuation and communication plans, you equip yourself with the tools to survive and thrive in seismic environments. Earthquakes are unpredictable, but with the right knowledge and planning, you can turn a potentially life-threatening event into a manageable situation that you and your group are fully prepared to face.

BOOK 22
HURRICANE PREPAREDNESS

Hurricanes are among the most destructive natural disasters, bringing intense winds, heavy rains, and flooding that can devastate landscapes and communities. In wilderness survival, preparing for such events requires a combination of strategic planning, building storm-resistant shelters, and ensuring the safety of essential resources. This chapter provides a comprehensive guide to hurricane preparedness, covering how to build shelters that withstand extreme conditions, creating safe zones during hurricanes, and stockpiling and protecting resources against flooding. By understanding these methods, you can better navigate and survive the chaos of hurricanes, ensuring both your safety and the protection of your vital supplies.

BUILDING SHELTERS RESISTANT TO STORMS

Constructing a shelter capable of withstanding hurricane-force winds and heavy rain is crucial for surviving these powerful storms. Hurricanes can bring sustained winds of over 100 miles per hour (160 km/h) and torrential downpours that cause flash floods, so it's essential to build a structure that offers both stability and protection against the elements.

Choosing a Safe Location

The location of your shelter is the first and most critical decision in building a storm-resistant structure. Avoid low-lying areas, floodplains, or places near rivers and streams, as these are prone to severe flooding during hurricanes. Instead, look for elevated ground, preferably on a slight incline, to help direct water flow away from the shelter.

Additionally, avoid building near large trees or loose rock formations that could become hazards during high winds. Hurricanes often bring down trees and cause landslides, so placing your shelter in a clear area reduces the risk of being struck by falling debris.

If you're near the coast, move as far inland as possible to minimize the impact of storm surges. Coastal areas are particularly vulnerable, and even small rises in sea level can inundate large areas with water. Prioritize building your shelter far enough inland and at a high elevation to escape the worst of the storm surge.

Constructing the Shelter Framework

When building a hurricane-resistant shelter, it's important to create a strong and flexible framework. A dome-shaped structure is ideal, as it presents less surface area for the wind to push against compared to flat or angular designs. This design also helps water flow off the structure, preventing pooling and reducing the risk of leaks.

Use sturdy wood or bamboo for the framework, materials that are both strong and have some flexibility, which allows them to bend rather than break under stress. Reinforce the joints with ropes or natural cordage to create a unified, solid structure that can move with the wind rather than resist it. Cross-bracing is essential for reinforcing the walls and roof, distributing force evenly and reducing the likelihood of collapse.

For the roof, use overlapping layers of large leaves (such as palm fronds) or tarp material if available. Angle the roof steeply to encourage water runoff. Adding layers of mud or clay can help insulate the roof and provide some additional weight to keep the structure grounded in strong winds.

Anchoring the Shelter

Anchoring is critical for keeping your shelter intact during a hurricane. Drive long stakes deep into the ground at the base of the shelter's support poles. Use ropes or vines to tie the structure securely to these stakes. If you have access to sandbags or large rocks, place them around the base of the shelter to provide extra weight and stability, anchoring the structure against high winds and floodwaters.

It's also wise to dig a drainage ditch around the perimeter of the shelter. This ditch channels water away, preventing it from pooling and weakening the ground beneath the structure. In a heavy downpour, this can be the difference between staying dry or having your shelter flooded and undermined.

Reinforcing an Existing Structure

If you're sheltering in an existing structure, such as a cabin or a makeshift dwelling, reinforce it by boarding up windows with wood planks or debris and bracing doors with additional support beams. Seal gaps in walls or the roof with mud, clay, or any available waterproof material to prevent leaks.

Create interior supports by placing poles or sturdy branches at key points inside the structure to provide additional reinforcement. These supports help absorb and distribute the force of high winds, reducing the strain on walls and the roof.

CREATING SAFE ZONES DURING HURRICANES

Even with a well-built shelter, hurricanes are unpredictable, and it's essential to establish safe zones both inside and outside your structure where you can take refuge if conditions worsen. Safe zones are areas designed to provide protection from wind, flooding, and falling debris, and they can be lifesaving when the storm intensifies.

Designing an Internal Safe Zone

Inside your shelter, designate a space that offers the most protection from the wind and falling debris. The ideal safe zone is an interior corner or an area away from windows and doors, which are the most vulnerable points in any structure. Reinforce this area with additional materials like rocks, logs, or sandbags to create a barrier that shields you from debris if the shelter's walls begin to weaken.

If possible, create a low, central spot in the shelter where you can huddle down. This position offers the most protection if the roof or walls collapse, as it reduces your exposure to falling objects. Keeping emergency supplies like a flashlight, first aid kit, and emergency food in this safe zone ensures that you have essentials on hand if you need to stay put for an extended period.

Establishing an Outdoor Safe Zone

In the event that your shelter becomes compromised or unsafe during the storm, you should have a designated outdoor safe zone as an alternative. This zone should be an open area, far from trees, cliffs, or other structures that could collapse or send debris flying. An open field or a clearing at a higher elevation is ideal, as it minimizes the risk of flooding and provides a relatively safe space from high winds.

When establishing this safe zone, prepare it by clearing any loose objects or debris that could become projectiles. If you have time before the storm hits, dig a shallow trench or low wall to provide some protection against strong winds and flying debris. This trench can also serve as a temporary shelter if you need to lie low and protect yourself from the elements.

Planning for the Worst: Safe Routes and Evacuation

Having an escape plan is essential in hurricane preparedness. If the conditions become too dangerous or if the shelter starts to collapse, it's critical to have pre-planned routes to higher ground or safer areas. These routes should be free of obstacles like rivers or low-lying areas that may flood during the hurricane.

If you're near a coast or in a floodplain, plan to evacuate to higher ground long before the hurricane reaches its full intensity. Avoid routes that pass through forests or near cliffs, as high winds and saturated soil can cause trees and rocks to fall. Practice these routes with your group or family, so everyone is familiar with the safest paths and knows where to regroup if separated.

STOCKPILING AND PROTECTING RESOURCES AGAINST FLOODING

Stockpiling supplies and protecting them against potential flooding is crucial for hurricane preparedness. A hurricane can isolate you for days or weeks, so having a secure supply of food, water, and other essential resources is necessary for survival. Properly storing these supplies ensures that they remain usable even if your shelter is damaged or flooded.

Building a Raised Storage System

Floodwaters are a major threat during hurricanes, so creating a raised storage system is essential for keeping supplies safe and dry. Use natural materials like logs or rocks to build a platform elevated at least two feet above the ground. This elevation helps protect against water damage and keeps supplies out of reach from small animals or pests.

Store food, water, and other supplies in waterproof containers if possible. Plastic barrels or tightly sealed plastic bins work well for this purpose. If these are not available, wrap supplies in waterproof materials such as tarps, ponchos, or heavy-duty garbage bags. Securing these containers tightly to the raised platform with ropes or bungee cords prevents them from being swept away by wind or water.

Stockpiling Essential Resources

In preparation for a hurricane, prioritize stockpiling the following essentials:

- Non-perishable food: Canned goods, dried fruits, nuts, rice, and beans are all long-lasting and provide necessary nutrients during emergencies.
- Water storage: Collect and store water in large containers, ensuring you have enough to last several days. Water purification tablets or filters are essential for treating water if your main supply becomes contaminated.
- Medical supplies: A well-stocked first aid kit with bandages, antiseptics, pain relievers, and any necessary prescription medications is critical.
- Fire-making tools: Lighters, waterproof matches, or fire starters help maintain warmth and prepare food, especially if power sources are disrupted.

Having these supplies secured and accessible means you are prepared to survive the immediate storm and its aftermath, even if you are isolated for a prolonged period.

Protecting Firewood and Fuel

If your shelter relies on firewood or other fuel sources for cooking and warmth, it's crucial to protect these resources against rain and flooding. Build a firewood stack off the ground using a wooden or stone platform. Cover the stack with a tarp, securing it tightly to keep the wood dry.

If you have access to fuel like propane, store it in sealed containers and secure them above ground level, ensuring they are safely out of reach of rising water. A secondary supply of tinder and kindling stored in waterproof bags can help you start a fire quickly, even if conditions are wet and windy.

MANAGING FLOOD RISKS AND PROTECTING SHELTER ENTRANCES

Flooding is one of the most severe risks during a hurricane, and taking proactive measures to protect your shelter's entrances is essential. Create barriers around doorways and openings using sandbags or heavy stones to prevent water from entering. If sandbags are not available, use logs, earth, or other natural materials to form a barrier.

Ensure that drainage ditches around your shelter are dug deep enough to channel water away efficiently. Keep these ditches clear of debris to allow water to flow freely and minimize the risk of pooling. If the shelter begins to flood, have a sump area—a low point where water can collect safely until it can be drained or removed.

RECOVERING AFTER THE HURRICANE

Once the storm has passed, the focus shifts to recovery. Assess the condition of your shelter carefully, checking for structural damage, water infiltration, and debris. Avoid entering any building or shelter that appears unstable, as it may collapse unexpectedly.

If your shelter is still intact, begin drying out any wet supplies and reinforce the structure to protect against potential after-effects, such as additional storms or weakening from flood damage. If the shelter is compromised, move to a safer location and begin constructing a temporary structure.

Check on your food and water supplies, ensuring they are still safe for consumption. Use water purification methods to treat any questionable water sources, and ration food carefully if you are unsure when conditions will improve.

CONCLUSION

Hurricanes are among the most formidable natural disasters, but with careful preparation, strategic planning, and the right survival techniques, you can greatly enhance your chances of weathering the storm. By building storm-resistant shelters, establishing safe zones, and stockpiling and protecting essential resources, you create a comprehensive approach to hurricane survival. This knowledge empowers you to not only withstand the initial impact of a hurricane but also adapt and thrive in its aftermath, turning the wilderness into a secure and resilient environment even in the face of nature's most extreme forces.

BOOK 23

COLD WEATHER SURVIVAL

Surviving in cold weather, especially in snowy and frigid conditions, requires a combination of specialized skills and knowledge. The wilderness becomes harsher and more demanding as temperatures drop, and the risks of hypothermia, frostbite, and dehydration increase. Understanding how to build insulated shelters, maintain body heat without fire, and find food in such environments is essential. This chapter delves into techniques for building winter shelters, staying warm using alternative methods, and locating and storing food in snowy conditions, ensuring that you can survive and thrive even in the coldest climates.

BUILDING INSULATED WINTER SHELTERS

Building a proper shelter in a cold environment is one of the most critical skills for winter survival. An effective winter shelter must protect you from wind, retain body heat, and provide insulation from the cold ground. Several types of shelters are suitable for winter conditions, each with its own advantages depending on available materials, snow conditions, and the duration of your stay.

The Importance of Location

Before building a shelter, choosing the right location is essential. Look for areas that provide natural windbreaks, such as dense tree lines, large boulders, or hills. Avoid open fields or exposed hilltops where wind can carry away heat and blow snow into your shelter. Equally important, steer clear of depressions or low-lying areas where cold air tends to settle and where you may be exposed to additional hazards, such as avalanches or flooding from melting snow.

If you are in a forested area, trees can provide natural coverage and support for building a shelter. Coniferous trees are particularly useful as their branches can be used for insulation and support. Additionally, building near a dense group of trees can provide protection from snow drifts and reduce wind exposure.

Constructing a Quinzee

A quinzee is one of the most effective snow shelters for winter survival. This structure is essentially a large mound of snow that is hollowed out to create a warm, insulated space. To build a quinzee:

1. Pile Snow: Start by piling snow into a large mound about 7-8 feet high and 10-12 feet in diameter. The snow should be well-packed to create a solid structure. This process can take time, so be prepared to work steadily, using a shovel or even your hands.

2. Let it Settle: After building the mound, let it settle for at least an hour. This allows the snow to bond and harden, making it easier to carve out without collapsing.
3. Hollow Out the Interior: Begin digging out the inside of the mound, creating a space large enough for you to sit up and lie down comfortably. The walls should be about 12 inches thick for insulation. Carve out a small entrance and create a raised platform inside where you can sleep, keeping your body elevated above the cold ground.
4. Ventilation: Poke a small hole in the roof to allow for ventilation, preventing carbon dioxide buildup. This hole is crucial for safety, as it ensures a continuous flow of fresh air.

Quinzees are effective because the compacted snow acts as an insulator, trapping body heat and protecting against wind. However, they require careful construction to avoid collapse and should be built well before nightfall.

Building a Tree Well Shelter

Another option in deep snow and forested areas is the tree well shelter. Tree wells are depressions that form around the bases of trees as snow accumulates on the branches above. These naturally occurring formations can be used as the foundation for a shelter:

1. Select a Tree: Choose a large coniferous tree with branches that extend outward, providing coverage above the well.
2. Dig Out the Well: Dig deeper into the tree well to create more space, forming a cavity that is large enough to sit or lie down in. Pack the walls with snow for added insulation.
3. Add Branches for Insulation: Line the ground with pine branches or other available foliage to insulate your body from the cold ground. Use more branches to create a roof that extends out from the tree trunk, shielding the opening.
4. Create a Ventilation Hole: As with any snow shelter, it's crucial to poke a hole through the roof to allow air circulation.

Tree well shelters are quicker to build than quinzees and can be effective temporary shelters. However, they offer less insulation and protection from wind, so they are best suited for shorter stays or emergency situations.

STAYING WARM WITHOUT FIRE

In some cold weather situations, building a fire may not be possible due to a lack of resources, high winds, or safety concerns. Knowing how to stay warm without fire is an essential survival skill that can keep you alive when other options are not available.

Layering Clothing Effectively

Properly layering your clothing is the most effective way to retain body heat without fire. The key is to use the three-layer system:

1. Base Layer: This layer should be made of moisture-wicking materials like wool or synthetic fabrics. Its purpose is to keep your skin dry by moving sweat away from your body.
2. Insulating Layer: The second layer, often made of fleece or down, traps warm air close to your body, providing insulation. This layer should be thick but still allow for movement.

3. Outer Layer: The final layer is a waterproof and windproof shell that protects against the elements. It should be breathable to prevent moisture buildup inside.

By adjusting these layers as your activity level changes, you can regulate your body temperature effectively, preventing sweating (which can lead to rapid cooling) and retaining warmth.

Using Body Heat and Insulated Sleeping Systems

When fire is not an option, maximizing your body heat is crucial. Sleeping systems designed for cold weather should include insulated sleeping pads and high-quality sleeping bags rated for low temperatures. The sleeping pad insulates you from the ground, while the sleeping bag traps body heat.

If you do not have a sleeping bag, use available materials to create insulation. Layers of pine boughs or dry leaves can be used to form a mattress and blanket that insulate your body. Additionally, huddle together with others if you are in a group; shared body heat significantly increases warmth.

Staying Active

Movement generates body heat, so staying active is another way to maintain warmth without fire. Simple exercises such as jumping jacks, push-ups, or running in place help boost circulation and raise body temperature. Be cautious not to overexert yourself, as sweating can lead to rapid heat loss once you stop moving.

If possible, alternate periods of movement with periods of rest, allowing your body to maintain a stable temperature. Avoid sitting or lying directly on the ground, as direct contact with cold surfaces draws heat away quickly.

FINDING AND STORING FOOD IN SNOWY CONDITIONS

Finding food in snowy, cold environments is challenging, as the landscape changes drastically with the season. Knowing where to look for food and how to store it properly in such conditions is crucial for long-term survival.

Foraging for Edible Plants

Even in snowy conditions, some edible plants can be found. Look for pine trees, as their needles can be brewed into a vitamin-rich tea. Pine nuts, if available, provide a valuable source of protein and fat. Also, search for lichen, which can be boiled to make it more palatable and digestible. Birch bark is another option that can be consumed after being stripped and boiled, providing carbohydrates.

When foraging, ensure you can positively identify the plants or materials you collect, as many lookalikes may be toxic, especially in winter when some identifying features may be hidden by snow.

Hunting and Trapping for Protein

In winter, animals may be less active, but tracks in the snow make it easier to identify their presence. Set up snares or deadfall traps along trails where you find evidence of small game such as rabbits, squirrels, or birds. These animals remain active during winter and provide essential protein and fat, which are crucial for maintaining body warmth and energy levels.

Fishing is another option if you are near a frozen lake or river. Look for areas where the ice is thinner or where water remains accessible, and use makeshift spears or lines to catch fish. Ice fishing requires patience and careful preparation, but fish can be an excellent source of nutrition in winter.

Storing Food in Cold Environments

Storing food in cold environments presents both opportunities and challenges. On one hand, the cold acts as a natural refrigerator, keeping meat and other perishables fresh for extended periods. However, food must be stored properly to avoid attracting wildlife or becoming frozen solid, which can make it difficult to consume.

Use natural snowbanks as makeshift freezers, but build food caches elevated off the ground using tree branches or rock platforms to prevent animals from reaching them. Wrap food in insulating materials like cloth or leaves before storing it to protect it from frost damage.

CONCLUSION

Cold weather survival requires a unique set of skills and knowledge, focusing on building effective shelters, maintaining body heat without fire, and finding and storing food in harsh conditions. By mastering these techniques, you can increase your chances of surviving and thriving in snowy and frigid environments, transforming the cold wilderness from a place of danger into a livable, manageable space.

BOOK 24
HOT WEATHER SURVIVAL

Surviving in extreme heat poses challenges very different from those encountered in cold weather environments. High temperatures, arid landscapes, and the risk of dehydration or heat-related illnesses all require specialized strategies to ensure safety and well-being. This chapter focuses on building shelters that protect against intense heat, conserving water in dry environments, and preventing and managing heat-related illnesses. By understanding these techniques, you can navigate the challenges of hot weather survival and stay safe in some of the harshest conditions on earth.

SHELTER BUILDING FOR EXTREME HEAT

In hot weather, shelter is essential not just for rest but for protection from the sun's intense rays. A well-built shelter provides shade, reduces the risk of dehydration, and helps regulate body temperature by creating a cooler environment. The following strategies and designs are effective for building shelters that offer relief from extreme heat.

Choosing the Right Location

When building a shelter in a hot environment, location is crucial. Look for natural features like large rocks, hills, or trees that provide shade and protection from direct sunlight. If you're in a desert or open area with little natural cover, prioritize finding a location that is elevated slightly to catch any breeze, as air movement helps cool the body.

Avoid building on sand dunes or rocky outcrops that absorb and retain heat, as these can create hot surfaces that amplify the surrounding temperature. Instead, aim for shaded spots or flat, open areas where you can create shade using natural or improvised materials.

Building a Desert Shelter

In arid or desert environments, creating a sun shelter is critical. One of the most effective and simple designs is the lean-to shelter, which can be constructed using minimal resources:

1. Collect Materials: Use branches, rocks, or other sturdy materials as the framework. If you don't have a tarp, improvise with large leaves, grasses, or any available cloth to create a covering.
2. Orient the Shelter: Position the lean-to so that it blocks the sun during the hottest part of the day (usually from late morning to mid-afternoon). Make sure it faces away from the direction of the prevailing winds to allow airflow but still provide protection from blowing sand.
3. Elevate the Roof: Set the roof at an angle to allow air circulation underneath. Keeping the

roof elevated not only provides shade but also lets hot air escape, creating a cooler micro-environment beneath.

For longer stays or in situations where more resources are available, you can build a dome-shaped shelter using branches and palm fronds. The dome shape provides stability and allows for air circulation, making it an effective way to reduce heat buildup.

Using the Earth for Insulation

The earth itself can be a powerful insulator in hot climates. Dugout shelters, for instance, involve digging shallow pits or trenches and covering them with vegetation, tarps, or other materials. The ground retains a cooler temperature than the air during the day, so lying directly on the ground or creating a below-ground shelter can significantly reduce heat exposure.

To build a dugout shelter:

1. Dig a Shallow Pit: The pit should be deep enough for you to sit or lie down comfortably. Avoid going too deep, as it may increase the risk of encountering reptiles or scorpions.
2. Create a Roof: Use branches, leaves, or available tarps to create a roof over the pit, providing shade. Make sure there is enough ventilation to allow for air circulation.

These shelters are particularly effective when combined with natural shade from vegetation or rocks, enhancing the cooling effect.

WATER CONSERVATION TECHNIQUES IN ARID ENVIRONMENTS

Water is the most vital resource in hot climates, and conserving it is essential for survival. In arid environments, every drop counts, so understanding how to find and conserve water is critical.

Finding Water Sources

In hot environments, natural water sources may be scarce. However, certain strategies can increase your chances of locating water:

• Follow Animal Tracks: Animals often travel to water sources, so tracking their movements can lead you to water. Look for converging paths that may indicate a trail to a hidden water source like a spring or oasis.

• Seek Out Greenery: Vegetation is often a sign of water, even in deserts. Plants like reeds, willows, or palms may grow near underground water. Digging in the vicinity of such vegetation may yield water.

• Collect Morning Dew: Use cloths to wipe dew from plants in the early morning. Squeeze the water into a container. While this method doesn't provide a lot of water, it can help supplement your supply.

Water Conservation Strategies

Once you have located water, conserving it becomes paramount. The following methods help minimize water loss:

1. Drink in Small Sips: Rather than gulping water, take small sips throughout the day to keep hydrated while conserving your supply.
2. Avoid Overexertion: Activity increases sweat production and water loss. Plan your tasks for cooler times, such as early morning or evening, and rest during the hottest part of the day. If you need to travel, do so at dawn or dusk to minimize exertion.
3. Cover Your Skin: Wear long sleeves and loose, light-colored clothing to protect your skin from the sun and reduce sweat evaporation. Covering your head with a cloth or hat also helps retain moisture and cool the body.

Creating Solar Stills

A solar still can be a lifesaver in hot, arid conditions, especially if there is no immediate water source. To create a solar still:

1. Dig a Hole: Dig a small hole in the ground and place a container at the bottom.
2. Line the Hole with Greenery: If available, place green plants around the container to increase the moisture content.
3. Cover the Hole with Plastic: Place a plastic sheet over the hole, securing the edges with rocks or soil. Weigh down the center with a small rock, so the plastic forms a cone shape above the container.
4. Collect Condensation: As the sun heats the ground, moisture will evaporate, condense on the plastic, and drip into the container. This method provides small amounts of distilled water throughout the day.

PREVENTING HEAT-RELATED ILLNESSES

Heat-related illnesses, such as heat exhaustion and heatstroke, are serious threats in hot environments. Understanding how to prevent and treat these conditions is vital for survival.

Recognizing the Signs

The first step in preventing heat-related illnesses is recognizing the early signs:

- Heat Exhaustion: Symptoms include heavy sweating, dizziness, nausea, and weakness. If untreated, heat exhaustion can lead to heatstroke.

- Heatstroke: This is a life-threatening condition where the body's temperature regulation fails. Symptoms include confusion, rapid pulse, dry skin, and loss of consciousness.

Preventive Measures

To avoid heat-related illnesses:

1. Stay Hydrated: Drink water regularly, even if you don't feel thirsty. Maintaining hydration helps regulate body temperature.
2. Find Shade: Avoid direct sun exposure by staying in shaded areas or inside your shelter during peak heat hours.
3. Use Cooling Techniques: Wet cloths and wrap them around your neck or wrists to cool your body. Splashing water on your skin also helps evaporative cooling.

Emergency Treatment

If someone shows signs of heatstroke, take immediate action:

- Move them to a shaded or cooler area.
- Douse them with cool water or place wet cloths on their body.
- Hydrate them if they are conscious and able to drink.
- Fan them to speed up the cooling process.

CONCLUSION

Surviving in extreme heat requires specific strategies focused on creating shelter, conserving water, and preventing heat-related illnesses. By understanding these techniques, you can navigate arid and desert environments with confidence, ensuring that you stay cool, hydrated, and safe in some of the most challenging conditions nature can present.

BOOK 25
LONG-TERM SUSTAINABILITY IN THE WILDERNESS

Surviving in the wilderness for an extended period requires more than just knowledge of basic survival skills; it necessitates a deep understanding of how to live sustainably within nature's limits. Unlike short-term survival, where you might rely heavily on quickly gathered resources or expedient techniques, long-term survival demands a strategic, balanced approach that ensures resources are managed wisely, habitats remain undisturbed, and ecosystems are maintained for continual support. This chapter focuses on the essential practices needed to achieve long-term sustainability, including how to rotate resources to prevent depletion, live in harmony with local flora and fauna, and create a self-sustaining camp setup that supports life over the long haul.

ROTATING RESOURCES TO PREVENT DEPLETION

A critical aspect of long-term wilderness survival is learning to manage resources in a way that ensures they remain available over time. Depletion of resources can lead to food shortages, environmental degradation, and ultimately, failure to sustain oneself in the wild. The key is to rotate resources and harvest responsibly, ensuring that ecosystems are given time to recover and continue providing essential support.

Understanding the Cycles of Nature

The first step in resource rotation is understanding the natural cycles and rhythms of the environment you inhabit. Every ecosystem has its unique timing for when plants grow, animals migrate, and water sources are most abundant. Observing and learning these patterns is crucial. For example, if you're located in a forested region, certain edible plants and fungi appear during specific seasons. Wild garlic and mushrooms, for example, might be abundant in spring but disappear during the summer months. By familiarizing yourself with these cycles, you can plan when and where to gather resources.

Applying this understanding, you must also become familiar with the reproductive cycles of plants and animal breeding seasons. Overharvesting or overhunting during these critical periods can deplete populations and prevent renewal. For instance, certain fish species lay eggs during specific times of the year; fishing during these spawning periods could disrupt their reproduction cycle and diminish future supplies. Similarly, gathering all the edible fruits from a bush can prevent it from spreading its seeds for the next season.

By being selective and timing your harvests, you ensure that both plants and animal populations have the opportunity to regenerate. Practicing such sustainable methods not only benefits the immediate environment but also creates a steady, ongoing supply of essential resources, allowing you to remain self-sufficient for the long term.

Establishing Rotational Harvesting Techniques

Once you have an understanding of the natural cycles, the next step is to implement rotational harvesting techniques. The concept is similar to crop rotation in agriculture: you use different areas for gathering resources at different times to allow previously harvested locations time to recover. For instance, if you identify multiple locations rich in wild herbs, you might gather from only one area at a time. This allows other areas to regrow and ensures that you do not deplete any one spot completely.

When fishing or hunting, practice the same rotation. Fish in different sections of a river or lake to prevent overfishing in one spot. Similarly, when hunting small game, avoid repeatedly hunting in the same area; instead, move between different territories, giving animal populations the chance to stabilize. Keeping a journal or log of your harvesting activities helps track which areas are currently in use and when to return to them.

Ensuring Soil and Water Health

Sustainability also involves maintaining the health of the soil and water sources in your environment. For example, when gathering roots or tubers, take only what is necessary and leave parts of the plants or tubers behind. Replanting parts of the root can promote regrowth, ensuring that these plants remain available in the future. In fishing, refrain from polluting water sources with waste or contaminants that could disrupt aquatic ecosystems.

Practices like no-till gardening can be applied even in the wilderness to maintain soil health. By only taking what is needed and leaving the environment as undisturbed as possible, you can help keep the soil fertile, enabling plants to regrow and ensuring that the area remains productive for an extended period.

LIVING IN HARMONY WITH LOCAL FLORA AND FAUNA

Achieving long-term sustainability means more than just taking from the environment—it requires living in a way that supports and enhances local ecosystems. This involves understanding the relationships between the flora and fauna in the area, ensuring that your activities do not disrupt the balance that nature has established over generations.

Understanding Local Plant Life

Knowledge of local plants is essential for living sustainably. This includes knowing which plants are edible, which have medicinal properties, and which are useful for building materials or other purposes. However, beyond merely identifying plants, understanding their role in the ecosystem is key. For instance, some plants are vital food sources for wildlife, while others play an important role in soil health or act as natural deterrents to pests.

Foraging practices should always be done with care and respect for these roles. If a plant is a critical source of nectar for bees or other pollinators, avoid overharvesting it. Instead, take small amounts from each plant and leave the majority to continue supporting the ecosystem. Similarly, if certain plants are invasive or harmful to the environment, removing them can be beneficial, creating space for native species to thrive.

Coexisting with Animals

Animals are an integral part of any wilderness environment, and understanding their behavior and needs is crucial for long-term survival. Observing animals can provide valuable information about food sources, water availability, and potential dangers. For instance, if you notice animals frequenting a particular area, it might indicate the presence of a water source or a supply of edible plants. However, this also means that you should be careful not to disturb these areas excessively.

When hunting, aim to take only what you need and avoid targeting species that are critical for the balance of the ecosystem. For example, predatory animals like wolves or eagles help control the populations of smaller animals; their absence could lead to an overpopulation of prey species, which in turn might overconsume vegetation and destabilize the ecosystem.

Supporting Biodiversity

One of the most effective ways to live in harmony with nature is by supporting and enhancing biodiversity. This can involve small but impactful actions like planting seeds from the fruits and plants you harvest, ensuring that these species continue to grow and spread. You can also create habitats for small animals and insects by leaving certain areas undisturbed or building simple shelters for birds or other creatures.

CREATING A SELF-SUSTAINING CAMP SETUP

For long-term survival, your camp must be designed not only to protect you from the elements but also to function in harmony with the environment. This involves creating systems for shelter, water, and food that are renewable and sustainable.

Constructing a Long-Term Shelter

Building a shelter that can withstand changing seasons and offer protection from various weather conditions is essential for sustainability. A log cabin or earth shelter can provide stability and insulation in cold weather, while a raised platform shelter may be suitable for wet or humid climates to avoid flooding and moisture buildup. Using natural, locally sourced materials like logs, clay, and stones ensures that your shelter blends with the environment and minimizes ecological impact.

Ensure your shelter is built with insulation in mind, using materials like moss, leaves, and clay to create thermal barriers that keep heat in during winter and cool air in during summer. A well-built shelter not only provides comfort but also reduces the need for energy-intensive solutions like constant fire usage for warmth, helping conserve resources.

Water Collection and Purification Systems

A self-sustaining camp setup must include a reliable and renewable water source. Establishing a rainwater catchment system with natural materials such as tarps or large leaves directs water into containers for storage. In regions with streams or rivers, creating a simple filtration system using sand, charcoal, and gravel ensures that the water remains potable without the need for constant boiling, which consumes resources like firewood.

In drier climates, solar stills or fog-catching nets can be constructed to collect small amounts of moisture from the air, supplementing your water supply during dry spells. Regular maintenance of these systems ensures that they continue to function effectively over the long term.

Cultivating a Food Garden

Growing your own food is a critical component of long-term sustainability. Depending on the environment, you can cultivate hardy plants like root vegetables (carrots, potatoes) and legumes (beans, peas) that require minimal maintenance but provide substantial nutrition. Creating raised beds or container gardens using natural materials allows you to grow food even in areas with poor soil.

Additionally, if your camp is situated near a water source, planting wild rice or other aquatic plants can provide an ongoing source of food. Foraging and farming should be balanced—plant seeds from gathered wild plants to create a small-scale but renewable food source that mirrors the surrounding environment's natural growth.

WASTE MANAGEMENT AND ENVIRONMENTAL CARE

Proper waste management is essential for maintaining a sustainable camp. Set up a composting system where organic matter, such as food scraps and plant waste, is converted into nutrient-rich soil for your garden. Avoid contaminating water sources by positioning latrines far from your main water source and covering waste regularly to minimize its impact.

By integrating these practices into your camp, you ensure that you live in balance with the environment, creating a setup that supports your needs while maintaining ecological harmony.

CONCLUSION

Long-term sustainability in the wilderness involves a careful balance of resource management, respect for local flora and fauna, and a self-sustaining camp setup. By learning how to rotate resources, live in harmony with nature, and establish renewable systems for food, water, and shelter, you build a resilient foundation for survival. This approach transforms wilderness survival from a temporary struggle into a sustainable, harmonious way of life that ensures both your survival and the health of the environment around you.

BOOK 26
TRACKING AND SCOUTING TECHNIQUES

Tracking and scouting are two of the most critical skills for surviving in the wilderness. Whether you are hunting game, locating water sources, or observing wildlife for safety, understanding how to read animal tracks, move stealthily through the environment, and establish safe observation points is essential. This chapter dives into these techniques, offering insights into recognizing animal tracks and movement patterns, scouting for resources without being detected, and creating observation points that provide security and information. Mastering these skills not only enhances your ability to gather food and resources but also ensures that you remain aware of your surroundings, minimizing the risks posed by predators or other threats.

RECOGNIZING ANIMAL TRACKS AND MOVEMENT PATTERNS

Reading animal tracks and interpreting movement patterns are foundational skills in tracking and scouting. Knowing what animal left a track, how recently it was made, and what the animal was doing at the time can provide you with valuable information about food sources, potential dangers, and the state of the environment.

Identifying Common Animal Tracks

Animal tracks vary significantly depending on the species, terrain, and weather conditions. Being able to identify these tracks accurately is the first step in effective tracking. Different animals leave distinct imprints; understanding these differences is crucial. For instance, deer tracks are heart-shaped, with two pointed ends indicating the direction of movement. They are often found near water sources or in open fields where deer graze. Bear tracks, on the other hand, show five distinct toe prints and usually have visible claw marks. They are larger and can be found near rivers where bears fish or forage for berries.

Predator tracks like wolves, coyotes, or mountain lions are often easy to distinguish by their size, shape, and the distance between prints. Wolves have oval-shaped tracks with four toes and claws visible, while mountain lions show rounded prints without claw marks, as they retract their claws while walking. Knowing these distinctions helps you identify not only the type of animal but also whether it might pose a threat or present an opportunity for hunting.

To determine how fresh a track is, examine its clarity and depth. Fresh tracks are crisp, with well-defined edges, while older tracks appear faded, filled with debris, or partially obscured by wind or rain. By understanding how to gauge the age of a track, you can estimate how close you are to the animal and whether it is worth pursuing.

Interpreting Movement Patterns

Tracks can tell you more than just the type of animal; they also reveal behavior and movement patterns. For instance, if you find tracks with even spacing and no signs of disturbance, the animal was likely walking or foraging. This indicates a calm, undisturbed environment. In contrast, tracks that show greater spacing or deep imprints may indicate that the animal was running, possibly fleeing from a predator or sensing danger.

Observing tracks in combination with other signs, such as broken branches, disturbed soil, or droppings, can provide additional context. If you notice that tracks lead to an area with chewed vegetation or scratch marks on tree trunks, it suggests the animal stopped to feed or mark its territory. Understanding these behaviors can guide your strategy—whether you are hunting, avoiding potential threats, or scouting for more information about the area.

In snowy environments, animal tracks are often more visible, but the snow can also distort or obscure them, making it challenging to determine freshness. Look for small details like crisp snow edges or snow kicked up from running animals to assess the situation. In sandy or muddy terrain, be mindful of drag marks that indicate the movement of animals with low bellies, such as snakes or certain reptiles, which may signal that these creatures are present in the area.

SCOUTING FOR RESOURCES WITHOUT BEING DETECTED

Scouting for food, water, and other essential resources is a crucial part of wilderness survival. However, it is just as important to move through your environment without being detected, whether by animals, other people, or potential threats. Stealth, caution, and observation skills are essential components of effective scouting, ensuring that you can gather resources safely and efficiently.

Practicing Stealth Movement

Stealth movement is a key aspect of scouting. Whether you're searching for water sources or hunting game, moving quietly and undetected increases your chances of success. The key is to walk softly and slowly, avoiding sudden movements that can draw attention or create noise. Avoid stepping directly on twigs, dry leaves, or other debris that may snap or crunch underfoot. Instead, try to place your feet on bare soil, soft moss, or grassy patches that absorb sound.

A technique called fox walking can be particularly effective. This method involves lowering your body's center of gravity by bending your knees and stepping lightly with the outer edge of your foot first, slowly rolling your foot inward until it touches the ground fully. By distributing your weight gradually, you reduce noise and minimize the risk of stepping on objects that might alert animals to your presence. This technique is especially useful when approaching water sources, where animals often congregate.

Use natural cover to your advantage. Move between bushes, rocks, and trees, ensuring that you remain hidden from view. In open areas, stay low and move quickly between points of cover. Observe your surroundings carefully before moving to the next position, looking for any signs of movement that might indicate the presence of animals or other humans.

Approaching Water Sources

Water sources are crucial targets when scouting for resources, as they often attract both animals and humans. However, they can also be risky locations, as they are hotspots for potential predators. When approaching a water source, always approach from downwind, ensuring that your scent does not carry to animals nearby. This approach reduces the likelihood of startling game and allows you to observe animal behavior before moving closer.

Look for signs of animal activity such as tracks, droppings, or worn trails leading to the water. These signs can give you valuable information about when and how animals use the area, helping you determine the best time to visit without risking detection. If you see fresh tracks or signs that animals are currently near the water, take note of the species and assess whether it poses any danger.

If the area is safe, use nearby vegetation for cover while you refill water containers or scout for other resources. Avoid making noise or disturbing the water surface, as this can alert nearby wildlife or other humans. If you suspect that predators or large animals are using the water source, retreat to a safe distance and observe from a hidden position until you are sure it is safe to proceed.

Scouting for Edible Plants and Game Trails

When scouting for food sources, patience and observation are key. If you're looking for edible plants, study the types of vegetation that grow in different environments and understand the specific signs that indicate their presence. For example, knowing that certain berry bushes thrive near streams or that wild onions grow in shaded areas can help you locate these resources more effectively.

When scouting for game, recognize and follow trails that animals use regularly. Game trails often appear as narrow paths with trampled grass, broken branches, or disturbed soil. Follow these trails slowly, observing the surroundings for additional signs like tracks, droppings, or fur caught on branches. By following these trails, you can locate areas where animals feed, rest, or drink, increasing your chances of finding reliable food sources.

Remain mindful of your visibility while following trails. Animals have heightened senses and can detect movement or smell from a distance. Stay downwind, move quietly, and use cover as you follow trails to avoid detection.

CREATING SAFE OBSERVATION POINTS

Establishing observation points allows you to monitor wildlife activity, scout for human presence, and assess your environment without exposing yourself to unnecessary risk. These observation points provide you with valuable information while keeping you concealed and protected.

Selecting the Right Vantage Point

The effectiveness of an observation point depends heavily on its location. Choose elevated positions like hilltops, large rocks, or tree platforms that offer a broad view of the surrounding area. Elevated positions allow you to scan for movement and identify patterns without being easily seen. However, it's essential to select positions that also provide cover—such as dense foliage, bushes, or rock formations—so that you remain hidden while observing.

If you cannot find an elevated location, use natural cover such as bushes or fallen logs to create a ground-level observation point. Make sure your view is unobstructed, allowing you to observe key areas like water sources, open fields, or game trails. From these positions, you can spot animals as they move through the area, gauge their habits, and plan your next moves accordingly.

Once you've chosen a vantage point, take note of multiple exit routes. In case you need to leave quickly due to the arrival of a predator or another threat, having several escape paths ensures your safety. Knowing your environment and having options for retreat is a fundamental aspect of wilderness scouting.

Creating Camouflaged Hides

Camouflaged hides are essential for effective observation in the wilderness. To build a hide, use natural materials like leaves, branches, and grass to blend into the environment. The key is to make the hide look as natural as possible. Avoid using brightly colored materials or unnatural shapes that could alert animals or people to your presence.

Construct the hide so that it provides cover from above, blocking the view of any aerial predators or individuals who might be passing by. Use a combination of vertical and horizontal coverage to ensure that you remain concealed from multiple angles. A well-built hide allows you to observe wildlife closely and safely, as animals are less likely to detect you when you are hidden within a natural structure.

These hides are particularly useful near areas where animals are likely to pass, such as game trails, water sources, or grazing fields. By positioning yourself strategically, you can gain insight into animal behavior, learning when and where different species are most active. This information can be invaluable for hunting or avoiding dangerous encounters.

The Importance of Patience and Silence

Scouting and observation require patience and discipline. Once you establish an observation point, remain as still and silent as possible. Avoid making sudden movements or noises that could draw attention to your location. If you need to reposition yourself, move slowly and deliberately, ensuring that you stay within cover.

Use binoculars, if available, to scan the area from your observation point. Focus on water sources, clearings, or known game trails, looking for any signs of movement. Watching animal behavior, such as how they approach water or interact with each other, can give you valuable clues about their routines and habits, informing your future scouting or hunting strategies.

If you're monitoring for human activity, look for signs such as smoke, unnatural noises, or disturbances in vegetation. Remaining undetected in these situations is paramount, so maintain your position and avoid revealing your presence. By staying patient and observant, you can gather the information you need without exposing yourself to unnecessary risks.

CONCLUSION

Tracking and scouting techniques are indispensable skills for wilderness survival, providing the knowledge and tools needed to navigate the environment, find resources, and stay safe. By learning to recognize animal tracks and movement patterns, moving stealthily through the landscape, and establishing safe observation points, you gain a deeper understanding of your surroundings and enhance your ability to thrive in the wild. These skills empower you to read the wilderness like a map, finding opportunities while avoiding threats, and ultimately turning the natural world into a resource-rich environment that supports long-term survival.

BOOK 27
BUILDING SIMPLE TOOLS AND WEAPONS

In the wilderness, having the skills to build tools and weapons from natural materials is essential for survival. Whether for hunting, protection, or crafting, simple implements like bows, arrows, spears, and stone tools can significantly enhance your ability to thrive in the wild. Building these tools requires a blend of ingenuity, patience, and an understanding of available resources. This chapter explores how to make primitive bows and arrows, craft spears and other defensive implements, and construct stone and bone tools, ensuring that you have the skills necessary to create the essential gear for survival.

MAKING PRIMITIVE BOWS AND ARROWS

The bow and arrow is one of the most effective hunting tools available in the wilderness. It provides a silent, long-range method for taking down game, allowing you to secure food without having to get dangerously close to your target. Constructing a primitive bow and arrows requires selecting the right materials, shaping them carefully, and understanding the mechanics of how they work together.

Selecting the Right Wood for a Bow

The first and most crucial step in making a bow is selecting the right wood. The wood must be strong, flexible, and capable of holding tension without snapping. Suitable types of wood for bow-making include yew, hickory, ash, and oak. These woods are known for their combination of toughness and flexibility, making them ideal for constructing durable, effective bows.

When selecting a piece of wood, look for a straight branch or sapling about your own height (approximately 5 to 6 feet long). It should be free of knots, cracks, and twists, as these imperfections can cause the bow to break under tension. The branch should also have a slight natural curve, which helps the bow maintain its shape and flexibility once it's strung.

Shaping the Bow

Once you have selected the wood, the next step is to shape it into a bow. Start by removing the bark and any small branches or knots. Use a knife or a sharpened stone to carve the stave (the main part of the bow) into a long, tapered shape. The bow's center, where the handle will be, should be thicker and more robust, while the limbs (the parts extending from the handle) should gradually taper to a thinner width. This tapering creates the necessary flexibility in the limbs to allow the bow to bend without breaking.

The bow must bend evenly, so work carefully, removing small amounts of wood at a time to maintain balance. A good way to check the balance is to slowly bend the bow, testing whether both limbs bend symmetrically. This process, known as tillering, involves continuous adjustments to ensure that the bow limbs curve evenly when drawn. If one side bends more than the other, you need to remove more wood from the opposite limb.

Crafting the Bowstring

The bowstring is another essential component of the bow. It must be strong and durable enough to withstand repeated tension without breaking. If you have access to modern materials like paracord or nylon, these make excellent bowstrings. However, in a primitive setting, natural materials such as plant fibers, animal sinew, or rawhide can be used effectively.

To create a bowstring from natural materials, twist fibers tightly together, ensuring the string is as uniform in thickness as possible. The twisting process binds the fibers, creating a strong, durable cord. Attach the string to the bow by cutting small notches at the tips of the bow's limbs and securing the string tightly within these notches. The string should be taut but not overly tight, allowing the bow to bend and store energy when drawn.

Crafting Arrows

With the bow completed, the next step is to craft arrows. Arrows require straight, lightweight wood, such as willow or dogwood branches. The ideal arrow shaft is about half the length of the bow and should be as straight as possible. Use a knife or sharp stone to smooth the shaft, removing any rough spots or branches that could affect the arrow's flight.

Sharpen one end of the arrow to a point, and if possible, harden it by briefly holding it over a flame. This process, known as fire hardening, strengthens the wood, making it more effective for piercing. If you have access to stone or bone fragments, you can attach these to the arrow's tip, creating a more lethal point. Use natural adhesives, like tree resin, combined with sinew or plant fibers to lash the point securely to the shaft.

To ensure the arrow flies straight, it needs fletching, which involves attaching feathers to the back end of the arrow. Use small bird feathers if available, splitting them and attaching them with sinew or plant fibers. The fletching helps stabilize the arrow during flight, improving accuracy and range.

CRAFTING SPEARS AND DEFENSIVE IMPLEMENTS

Spears are among the most versatile tools in the wilderness. They serve multiple purposes, including hunting, fishing, and self-defense. Crafting a spear involves selecting the right materials and shaping them for maximum effectiveness.

Making a Hunting Spear

To build a hunting spear, choose a long, straight branch or sapling. The wood should be as tall as you are or taller, and it should be lightweight yet sturdy enough to withstand impact. Suitable woods for spear shafts include ash, oak, or hickory, as they provide the strength needed for a durable spear.

Sharpen one end of the spear into a point using a knife or a sharp stone. If you have access to fire, harden the tip by holding it over the flames until it darkens slightly. This process not only hardens the wood but also makes the point more durable and less likely to splinter. A fire-hardened spear is effective for hunting both small and large game, allowing you to maintain distance from potentially dangerous animals.

For added effectiveness, attach a stone, bone, or metal tip if available. Lash the tip securely to the spear shaft using sinew, plant fibers, or rawhide strips. A spear with an attached point is far more effective for both thrusting and throwing, as it can penetrate deeper and with greater force.

Crafting a Fishing Spear

A fishing spear is a specialized tool designed to catch fish in shallow waters. To create one, start with a straight shaft, similar to a hunting spear, but modify the tip by splitting it into multiple prongs (three or four). Sharpen each prong to create a forked shape. These prongs increase the chance of spearing fish by providing a wider surface area.

Using a cord or sinew, tie the prongs to maintain their spread, ensuring they stay open while in use. A properly crafted fishing spear allows you to catch fish by thrusting it into the water quickly and efficiently. Practicing your aim in shallower waters before attempting in deeper or fast-moving areas improves your success rate.

Defensive Implements: Clubs and Shields

For self-defense, a club is one of the simplest and most effective weapons you can craft. Choose a thick, heavy branch—about 2 to 3 feet long—that feels comfortable to grip. The head of the club should be denser and thicker than the handle. If possible, add extra weight by embedding stones or metal fragments into the club's head using sinew or rawhide to secure them. A club like this can deliver significant force in close combat, making it a valuable tool for protection.

Another defensive tool is a shield, which can be crafted using bark, wood planks, or woven branches. Select a large piece of bark or a flat, broad section of wood, and shape it to cover your upper body. Reinforce it with sticks or branches, and if available, use leather or vines to strap it to your arm. A shield not only provides protection against animal attacks but can also be useful in deflecting thrown objects or blows from other humans.

CONSTRUCTING STONE AND BONE TOOLS

In the wilderness, having tools for cutting, shaping, and building is critical. Stone and bone tools are some of the most fundamental implements you can create, allowing you to fashion a variety of weapons, prepare food, and build shelters.

Making a Stone Knife

A knife is one of the most versatile and essential tools in the wilderness. To make a stone knife, look for hard stones like flint, chert, or obsidian, which can be shaped into sharp edges. The process of flintknapping—using another stone to chip away small flakes—allows you to create a blade with a sharp cutting edge.

Begin by finding a suitable stone that has a naturally flat surface. Hold it in one hand and use a second, smaller stone to strike it at an angle, chipping off flakes until you have a blade shape. This process takes patience and practice, but the result is a durable cutting tool. The blade can be used for a variety of purposes, including preparing food, cutting wood, or shaping other tools.

Once the blade is formed, attach it to a handle made from wood or bone. Use sinew or plant fibers to secure the blade to the handle, ensuring it is tightly bound for stability. This knife becomes a critical tool for everyday tasks, increasing your efficiency and survival prospects.

Crafting Stone Axes and Hatchets

A stone axe or hatchet is another vital tool that can be used for chopping wood, breaking bones, or building shelters. To create one, find a flat, heavy stone with one sharp edge. If the stone lacks a naturally sharp edge, you can use the flintknapping technique to shape it.

Once you have your stone blade, secure it to a wooden handle using sinew, rawhide, or plant fibers. The handle should be about 2 to 3 feet long, providing enough leverage for chopping. Creating a groove in the handle and fitting the stone blade into it before tying it down increases stability.

With a properly crafted stone axe, you can split wood, build shelters, and process large game, significantly increasing your efficiency in the wilderness.

Bone Tools: Needles, Fishhooks, and Scrapers

Bone is another valuable material for crafting small tools, especially when animals are hunted for food. Bones are lightweight, strong, and easy to carve into specific shapes, making them ideal for creating tools like needles, fishhooks, and scrapers.

To make a bone needle, choose a small, sturdy bone, such as a rib or leg bone from a bird or small mammal. Sharpen one end into a fine point, and carve a small hole or notch near the other end for threading cord or sinew. This needle can be used to stitch clothing, repair gear, or construct shelters using hide or fabric.

A bone fishhook is another essential tool. Carve a small bone into a hook shape, ensuring that the point is sharp and the end is barbed to hold onto fish. These hooks can be tied to a fishing line made from plant fibers or sinew, allowing you to fish efficiently in streams or lakes.

Finally, bone scrapers are useful for processing hides or preparing food. Carve a flat, sharp edge into a bone and use it to scrape fur or scales. These tools help you make the most of every part of an animal, minimizing waste and maximizing resources.

CONCLUSION

The ability to craft tools and weapons from natural materials is a cornerstone of wilderness survival. By learning to make primitive bows and arrows, spears, and stone tools, you equip yourself with the skills necessary to hunt, defend, and build effectively. These tools not only enhance your ability to thrive but also transform the wilderness into a place of opportunity, where every resource can be used to its fullest potential. Mastering these techniques ensures that you are prepared for any challenge nature presents, allowing you to not just survive, but truly adapt and succeed in the wild.

BOOK 28
BUSHCRAFT SKILLS

Bushcraft is a comprehensive set of skills that focuses on using natural materials and the environment to create tools, shelter, and amenities necessary for living comfortably in the wilderness. Unlike basic survival techniques, which often focus on short-term solutions, bushcraft emphasizes sustainable and practical skills that enable you to live in harmony with nature over an extended period. This chapter explores essential bushcraft skills, including weaving and basket-making with natural fibers, constructing camp furniture and storage solutions, and carving and whittling for practical use. Mastering these skills allows you to transform the natural environment into a source of sustainable comfort and efficiency, turning the wilderness into a home rather than a temporary refuge.

WEAVING AND BASKET-MAKING WITH NATURAL FIBERS

Weaving and basket-making are essential bushcraft skills that allow you to create tools and containers from natural fibers found in the environment. These skills not only provide you with storage solutions but also open up the possibility to craft clothing, fishing nets, and other items essential for survival and comfort. Learning to identify and use the right types of fibers is the first step in mastering these crafts.

Identifying Suitable Natural Fibers

The wilderness offers a variety of natural materials that can be used for weaving and basket-making. These materials must be strong, flexible, and abundant to be effective. Common plants and trees that provide suitable fibers include:

- Willow branches: Willow is a versatile plant that grows near water sources and offers long, flexible branches ideal for weaving baskets and making cordage.

- Cattails: Cattails, found in wetland areas, have strong, fibrous leaves that can be used for weaving mats, baskets, and even clothing.

- Birch bark: The inner bark of birch trees can be stripped off in long sheets and used for weaving containers, creating waterproof storage solutions.

- Reeds and grasses: Tall grasses and reeds are also great for weaving due to their flexibility and availability in many environments.

When gathering fibers, choose live, green materials whenever possible, as they are more pliable and easier to work with than dry, brittle ones. However, avoid taking too much from any one plant to prevent damage to the ecosystem.

Basic Weaving Techniques

To begin weaving, you first need to prepare the fibers. For example, with willow branches, soak them in water for a few hours to increase their flexibility. If you're using cattails or grass, strip them into thin, even strips. Once your materials are ready, you can start practicing basic weaving techniques:

1. Twining: This is a simple method where two strands are twisted around vertical stakes (called warps). Twining is ideal for creating tight, durable weaves suitable for baskets or mats.
2. Plaiting: Plaiting involves interlacing several strands of fiber over and under each other, similar to braiding hair. This technique is perfect for making flat items like mats, walls for shelters, or even simple clothing.
3. Coiling: Coiling is a technique where you wrap a long piece of fiber around itself, securing it with smaller strands as you go. This method is often used for making sturdy, round baskets or containers. Start with a small loop and continue coiling outward, securing each layer with the smaller strands until you reach the desired size.

Basket-Making

Baskets are one of the most useful items you can create with bushcraft weaving skills. They serve as storage for food, gathering containers for berries, and even as tools for carrying firewood or fish. To make a simple basket:

1. Create the Frame: Use several thick, sturdy pieces of willow or similar material as the vertical stakes (the warp). Arrange them in a circular pattern, securing them at the base by tying them with fiber or cordage.
2. Weave the Sides: Using a thinner, more flexible material like cattail leaves, begin weaving horizontally, alternating over and under each vertical stake. As you continue weaving, the structure will begin to take shape. Adjust the spacing between the stakes as needed to maintain a consistent pattern.
3. Finish the Basket: Once you've reached the desired height, fold the tops of the vertical stakes over the rim and weave them back into the structure for stability. This creates a finished edge and secures the weave. For additional strength, add a handle by attaching a bent branch across the top, securing it with cordage or plant fibers.

By mastering these basic weaving techniques, you can create a variety of useful items, from small storage baskets to larger fish traps and shelter mats, using only what nature provides.

CONSTRUCTING CAMP FURNITURE AND STORAGE SOLUTIONS

Constructing camp furniture and storage solutions using natural materials is a vital bushcraft skill that enhances your comfort and efficiency in the wilderness. By building simple yet functional items like tables, chairs, shelving, and raised platforms, you can create a more organized and livable campsite. These items also help keep your food and equipment off the ground, protecting them from moisture and animals.

Making a Camp Stool or Chair

A camp stool or chair is a simple and practical item that can be built using basic bushcraft skills. Sitting on a raised surface instead of the ground keeps you dry and comfortable, making everyday tasks more manageable. To build a camp stool:

1. Find Suitable Wood: Look for strong, straight branches or poles. You'll need three sturdy pieces for the legs (about knee height) and another three or four pieces to form the seat frame.
2. Create the Seat Frame: Using the shorter pieces, construct a triangle or square frame for the seat. Lash the corners together using natural cordage, such as vines, strips of bark, or plant fibers. Make sure the frame is stable and secure.
3. Attach the Legs: Lash the three long branches securely to the corners of the seat frame, ensuring they are evenly spaced and angled outward slightly for stability. Adjust as necessary until the stool stands upright and feels solid.
4. Weave the Seat: Use flexible materials like willow branches, reeds, or cattail leaves to create a woven seat. Weave the material back and forth across the frame, ensuring it is tight enough to support your weight.

This basic stool design can be modified into a larger chair by adding a backrest. Simply extend two of the legs upward and connect them with another horizontal piece to create support. Weave additional material between the backrest frame for comfort.

Building a Raised Sleeping Platform

Sleeping off the ground is essential in the wilderness to protect against moisture, cold, and crawling insects. A raised sleeping platform can be constructed using sturdy poles and natural cordage:

1. Select the Location: Choose a flat, even spot that is well-drained and away from tree roots or rocks. Ensure the area is protected from wind and rain, using natural windbreaks like rocks or dense foliage if available.
2. Build the Frame: Gather long, sturdy poles for the frame (about 6 feet in length for a single person). Arrange them in a rectangle and secure the corners with cordage. Make sure the frame is stable before proceeding.
3. Attach Cross Supports: Add smaller poles across the width of the frame to provide support for the sleeping surface. Space them evenly to create a sturdy platform.
4. Weave the Sleeping Surface: Use flexible branches or plant fibers to weave a surface over the frame, similar to how you would weave a basket. The weave should be tight and evenly spaced to provide a comfortable sleeping area.

A raised platform keeps you dry, warm, and safe from insects, making it a critical addition to any long-term camp setup.

Creating Shelves and Storage Solutions

Organizing your campsite with shelves and storage solutions improves efficiency and keeps supplies safe from animals and weather. Building a simple shelf involves securing a flat plank (or several branches tied together) between two trees or upright poles. You can also construct lean-to shelves by propping planks against a large rock or tree trunk and securing them with stakes and cordage.

If you need a food storage solution, a raised platform similar to the sleeping platform works well. Elevate the platform high enough to keep food safe from small animals and pests. Cover it with a woven mat or tarp to protect supplies from rain.

CARVING AND WHITTLING FOR PRACTICAL USE

Carving and whittling are essential bushcraft skills that allow you to create useful tools, utensils, and even small furniture items. From carving spoons and bowls to making tent pegs or tool handles, these skills transform raw wood into practical items that enhance your wilderness experience.

Selecting the Right Wood for Carving

Choosing the right type of wood is critical for carving. Softer woods like birch, cedar, or pine are ideal for beginners, as they are easier to shape with simple tools. Hardwoods like oak, ash, or maple are more durable but require more skill and patience. Always use freshly cut green wood when possible, as it is easier to carve than dry, seasoned wood.

Carving Basic Tools and Utensils

Spoons and Bowls: Carving simple utensils like spoons and bowls is a practical and rewarding bushcraft skill. To carve a spoon:

1. Select a Small Branch: Choose a straight, green branch that is about a foot long and has a diameter that matches the size of the spoon you want to carve.
2. Shape the Handle and Bowl: Use a knife to carve the general shape of the spoon, creating a flat handle and rounded bowl at the end. Take your time, gradually removing wood to form the shape.
3. Hollow Out the Bowl: Carefully carve out the bowl using a curved blade or a small stone tool, if available. Smooth the surface as much as possible to create a functional and comfortable utensil.

Tent Pegs and Tool Handles: These are simple but essential items for building and securing your camp. To make a tent peg:

1. Cut a Branch to Length: Choose a sturdy branch about 8-10 inches long.
2. Sharpen One End: Carve one end of the peg to a point for driving into the ground.

3. Notch the Other End: Create a small notch near the top for securing the tent rope or cordage. This ensures that the peg holds the structure securely.

Tool Handles: If you've created stone or bone tools, you'll need handles for better grip and control. Carve the handle to fit your hand comfortably, then use cordage to securely attach the tool head.

Advanced Carving: Making Decorative and Functional Items

Once you've mastered the basics, you can expand your carving skills to create more advanced and decorative items, such as cups, ladles, or even small furniture pieces like stools or shelves. These items not only serve practical purposes but also enhance the comfort and aesthetics of your camp. By investing time in crafting such items, you transform your temporary shelter into a functional and comfortable living space.

For instance, carving wooden hooks or hangers helps organize gear around the campsite. Carve a branch into a hook shape and secure it to a tree or structure. These hooks can hold cooking pots, bags, or clothing, keeping them off the ground and organized.

CONCLUSION

Bushcraft skills like weaving, constructing camp furniture, and carving tools are essential for transforming the wilderness into a home. By mastering these techniques, you can create the tools and structures needed to live comfortably and sustainably in nature. These skills enhance your efficiency, improve your safety, and allow you to build a more organized, efficient, and livable campsite. Whether crafting baskets for storage, building raised sleeping platforms, or carving spoons and tent pegs, bushcraft turns the wilderness into a resource-rich environment where everything you need can be crafted with your own hands.

BOOK 29
ADVANCED NAVIGATION TECHNIQUES

Advanced navigation techniques are essential for long-term wilderness survival, especially when you must navigate without the aid of modern technology like GPS or maps. Understanding how to track time and distance, read the landscape, and navigate through challenging terrains like dense forests and mountainous regions can be the difference between reaching safety or getting hopelessly lost. This chapter covers advanced skills needed to move confidently through the wilderness, helping you understand how to use the environment as your guide.

TRACKING TIME AND DISTANCE WITHOUT TECHNOLOGY

Without technological devices like GPS or clocks, tracking time and distance becomes a matter of observation, estimation, and knowledge of nature's rhythms. Learning these skills can greatly enhance your ability to stay oriented and on course, especially when navigating in unfamiliar or challenging terrain.

Tracking Time Using Natural Cues

Tracking time in the wilderness involves understanding the movement of the sun, the phases of the moon, and natural patterns that occur daily. Here are a few ways to gauge time without a watch:

1. Using the Sun: The sun's movement across the sky is the most reliable way to track time. The sun rises in the east and sets in the west, and its position at midday indicates the approximate time of noon. To estimate time during daylight hours, divide the sky into equal sections based on the sun's position:

• When the sun is low in the eastern sky, it is morning (6-9 AM).

• When it is high and directly above you, it is close to noon.

• As it moves lower in the western sky, it is afternoon to early evening (3-6 PM).

2. You can also use the shadow stick method. Place a stick upright in the ground and mark the tip of its shadow. As the sun moves, the shadow's position changes. When the shadow is shortest, it indicates midday. Tracking the shadow's movement over time helps you estimate the passage of hours.

3. Phases of the Moon: The moon's phases provide a rough estimate of time over weeks rath-

er than hours. A full moon appears approximately every 29.5 days. Knowing the current phase of the moon can help you determine the approximate date if you have already been tracking the passage of days.

4. Natural Rhythms: Observe nature for daily patterns that indicate time. Birds often start singing at dawn and become quieter during midday. Insects like crickets are more active in the early evening. Paying attention to these rhythms gives you clues about the time of day, even when the sun or moon is not visible due to cloud cover or dense forest canopy.

Estimating Distance Without Technology

Tracking distance in the wilderness without technology relies on physical cues and measurements related to your body. Here are some techniques:

1. Pacing Method: One of the most common ways to measure distance is by counting your steps, also known as pacing. First, measure the average length of your stride by walking a known distance (such as 100 feet) and counting your steps. This gives you a baseline measurement (e.g., 2 feet per step). Multiply the number of steps taken during your hike by the length of your stride to estimate the distance traveled. To keep an accurate count, use a simple method like picking up a small stone for every hundred steps or tying knots in a cord. Remember that terrain can affect your stride, so adjust your count if you are traveling uphill or downhill.

2. Time-Based Estimation: If you maintain a consistent pace, you can estimate distance based on the time spent walking. For instance, if you know you typically cover about 2 miles per hour on flat terrain, you can estimate that after one hour of travel, you have likely covered that distance. Adjust this calculation based on the terrain, reducing speed estimates for uphill or rocky paths.

3. Visual Landmarks: When estimating distance over long stretches, use visible landmarks. Estimate how far a distant landmark is based on known measurements. For example, if you know that a hill is about half a mile away and it takes you around 15 minutes to reach it at your normal pace, you can use this information as a reference point for estimating future distances. As you travel, check your progress against these visual markers to maintain a sense of how far you've gone.

READING THE LANDSCAPE AND ENVIRONMENTAL CLUES

Learning to read the landscape is crucial for effective navigation, as the terrain provides clues about direction, proximity to water, and changes in elevation. Understanding how to interpret these environmental signs helps you maintain your bearings and navigate effectively even in unfamiliar territory.

Understanding Terrain Features

Terrain features such as hills, valleys, ridges, and rivers act as natural navigation aids. By recognizing these features and understanding how they relate to each other, you can build a mental map of your environment:

1. Ridges and Valleys: Ridges and valleys are significant terrain features that indicate changes in elevation. When traveling, pay attention to the slope of the ground. If you're following a ridge, you'll often have higher ground on either side, and it can guide you in a consistent direction. Valleys, conversely, are lower areas often containing streams or rivers, and they typically lead to larger bodies of water or openings in the landscape. To navigate using ridges and valleys, aim to move along the ridgeline if you need an unobstructed view of the surrounding area. If you seek water or an easier path, follow a valley.

2. Waterways: Rivers, streams, and lakes are excellent guides for navigation. Water generally flows downhill and converges into larger bodies, leading you to lower elevations and, eventually, to sea level or larger lakes. If you find a stream, you can follow it downstream to find larger water sources, which might lead you to populated areas or safer camping spots.

3. Mountain Ranges: Mountains are prominent landmarks that can serve as directional beacons. If you know the general orientation of a mountain range (e.g., north-south or east-west), you can use it as a reference for maintaining your direction. When traveling in mountainous terrain, it is usually easier to navigate around the base rather than traversing over peaks unless necessary.

Using Vegetation as a Guide

Plants and trees are often aligned with specific environmental factors, and they can be used to help navigate:

1. Moss Growth: The myth that moss only grows on the north side of trees is not entirely accurate, but it is true that moss prefers shady, damp environments. In dense forests, moss is more likely to grow on the side of the tree that faces away from direct sunlight. In the northern hemisphere, this is often the north or east side, but always check multiple trees to confirm consistency.

2. Wind Patterns: Trees and vegetation are often shaped by prevailing winds. For example, in open areas or mountains, trees might lean or grow in a direction that indicates the dominant wind pattern. Understanding the local wind direction can give you an idea of orientation, especially when combined with other clues like the position of the sun.

3. Vegetation Changes: Changes in vegetation often indicate proximity to water. Lush, green plants or trees like willows and alders are commonly found near water sources. If you see these species, it's worth investigating further to locate a stream or pond, which can serve as a navigation aid.

NAVIGATING DENSE FORESTS AND MOUNTAINOUS TERRAIN

Navigating through dense forests or mountainous regions presents unique challenges. The lack of clear sightlines and the presence of obstacles like cliffs, thick underbrush, and uneven ground require specialized techniques for maintaining direction and ensuring safe passage.

Dense Forest Navigation

In dense forests, visibility is often limited, making it easy to become disoriented. Here are some strategies for navigating effectively:

1. Using a Directional Guide: Before entering a forest, establish a primary direction using the sun's position or other visible landmarks. This helps set your initial course. As you move into the forest, maintain this direction by using a compass if available or by observing how the sun filters through the canopy. If you don't have a compass, pay attention to other cues like shadows, tree growth patterns, or even the general slope of the land.
2. Blazing a Trail: Mark your path as you move through dense forest to avoid doubling back or getting lost. This can be done by breaking small branches, tying strips of cloth, or carving marks into tree trunks. These markers should be frequent enough to guide you back if needed but not so visible as to attract unwanted attention from wildlife or other people.
3. Maintaining Straight Paths: It is easy to veer off course when visibility is low. To keep a straight path, pick a distant tree or feature directly in front of you and walk toward it. Once you reach it, choose another feature ahead. This leapfrogging method keeps you moving in a relatively straight line, reducing the risk of veering off track.

Navigating Mountainous Terrain

Mountainous regions offer different challenges, including steep slopes, cliffs, and rapidly changing weather. Navigating this terrain requires a strategic approach:

1. Route Planning: Before ascending a mountain, plan your route by looking for natural ridgelines, valleys, or switchbacks that offer gradual inclines. Avoid steep, exposed slopes that are prone to rockfalls or avalanches. If you must climb, choose routes that offer natural handholds, such as areas with dense vegetation or rock formations.
2. Using Elevation as a Guide: Higher ground provides better visibility and allows you to assess the surrounding landscape. When navigating mountains, aim to ascend to a high point early in your journey to establish your bearings. From the summit or a high ridge, you can identify valleys, lakes, and other features that serve as navigation aids.
3. Weather Awareness: Mountain weather can change rapidly. Always be aware of the clouds and wind direction, as these can signal incoming storms or changes in temperature. In mountainous terrain, storms often approach from the west, so if you notice dark clouds forming in that direction, it's wise to seek shelter or descend to lower ground.

Reading the Ground for Safe Passage

When navigating through rough terrain, it's important to pay attention to the ground. Loose rocks, unstable slopes, and hidden crevices can pose dangers. Use the following techniques for safe movement:

1. Assessing Rock Stability: Before stepping on rocks or slopes, test the stability with your foot or a walking stick. Avoid areas where rocks shift easily or show signs of recent erosion.
2. Using Animal Trails: In mountainous areas, animals often create paths that follow the safest

and most efficient routes. These trails, which are usually worn and smooth, can be used as guides. However, remain cautious—predator trails might lead you into unsafe areas.

3. Traversing Slopes: When moving across slopes, use a zigzag pattern rather than going directly up or down. This switchback method reduces the strain on your body and prevents slipping, especially on loose terrain.

CONCLUSION

Advanced navigation techniques are essential for wilderness survival, enabling you to move confidently and safely through unfamiliar and challenging environments. By mastering the ability to track time and distance without technology, read the landscape for environmental clues, and navigate dense forests and mountainous terrains, you build the skills needed to maintain orientation and find your way. These techniques transform the wilderness from a place of uncertainty into a navigable, manageable environment where every step is taken with knowledge and confidence.

BOOK 30

WATER STORAGE AND CONSERVATION

Water is the most critical resource for survival in the wilderness. It is vital not only for hydration but also for cooking, hygiene, and sometimes even for building materials like mud or clay. However, securing a consistent and clean water supply can be a challenge, especially during droughts or in arid environments. In these situations, the ability to create water storage systems from natural materials, efficiently use limited water resources, and build rainwater collection systems becomes essential. This chapter explores these techniques in detail, providing a comprehensive guide to managing and conserving water in the wild, ensuring you have the skills to store, use, and collect this precious resource effectively.

CREATING WATER STORAGE SYSTEMS FROM NATURAL MATERIALS

In a survival situation, one of the first priorities is to establish a reliable way to store water. While modern containers like canteens or bottles are ideal, they may not always be available. Knowing how to create water storage systems using natural materials is a critical bushcraft skill that ensures you can collect and preserve water for when you need it most.

Identifying and Gathering Suitable Natural Materials

The first step in creating water storage systems is identifying the natural materials available in your environment. The key qualities needed for effective water storage materials include flexibility, impermeability, and durability. Some of the most effective natural resources for building water containers include:

- Gourds and Large Fruits: If you find wild gourds or other large fruits with hard shells, these can be hollowed out and dried to serve as water containers. Once dried, the gourd becomes a lightweight and portable vessel, perfect for carrying water over short distances. Be sure to seal any cracks or openings with natural resin or tree sap to prevent leaks.

- Bamboo: In tropical or subtropical environments, bamboo is an excellent resource for water storage. The hollow segments of bamboo can be cut and sealed at one end to create a container that can hold a significant amount of water. Bamboo is naturally strong and watertight, making it ideal for creating multiple water storage units that can be connected or carried individually.

- Animal Bladders and Stomachs: If you've hunted or scavenged an animal, you can use its bladder or stomach as a water storage pouch. Clean and dry these organs thoroughly before using them. They are flexible, lightweight, and can hold a surprising amount of water, making them useful for temporary storage.

- Tree Bark: In temperate and boreal forests, bark from trees such as birch or cedar can be used to create water-tight containers. Carefully remove a large section of bark and shape it into a cylinder or cone. Bind the edges together using natural cordage like vines or split roots, and seal any seams with pine resin to create a durable container.

Constructing Water Storage Containers

Once you have gathered suitable materials, constructing effective storage containers involves shaping and sealing them properly. For instance, if you're using bamboo, cut a section with at least one intact joint to form the base of the container. Clean the interior thoroughly and, if necessary, use heated stones to dry out any residual moisture, ensuring the bamboo does not rot.

For bark containers, peel the bark gently to avoid cracking. Shape it while it's still fresh and pliable, binding it securely with natural cordage. Heating pine resin or beeswax to seal the seams helps create a water-tight vessel. These containers can be placed in streams to collect water or used to store rainwater.

When using animal organs, such as a bladder, wash it with clean water and allow it to dry. Afterward, you can inflate it slightly to stretch the material, making it more suitable for holding liquids. Seal the opening with a tight knot or secure it with a small wooden stopper.

These methods provide you with a variety of water storage solutions, ensuring that you always have the means to collect and preserve water, even when modern containers are unavailable.

EFFICIENT USE OF WATER RESOURCES DURING DROUGHTS

In situations where water is scarce, managing and conserving every drop becomes crucial. Drought conditions or arid environments require advanced strategies for efficient water use. Understanding how to make the most of limited water resources can mean the difference between survival and dehydration.

Prioritizing Water Needs

The first step in efficient water management is prioritizing your needs. In a survival situation, drinking water takes precedence over all other uses. Your body needs a minimum of 2-3 liters per day to stay hydrated under normal conditions. During intense physical activity or in hot environments, this requirement can double. Therefore, make sure you always reserve the most water for drinking.

Other essential uses of water include cooking and hygiene. To conserve water during cooking, choose methods that minimize water usage, such as steaming food using small amounts of water that can be reused. When washing, use a small amount of water and avoid submerging your hands or face. Instead, wet a cloth and wipe down, reducing the amount needed.

Recycling Water and Minimizing Waste

Recycling water is an effective strategy when resources are scarce. For instance, graywater from washing can be repurposed for other tasks like cleaning tools or even watering plants in your camp's garden (if you have one). Make sure the graywater is not contaminated with chemicals or substances that could be harmful if reused.

If you are using water for cooking, save the water used to boil food like rice or pasta. This water is still useful for hydration, and the nutrients it absorbs during cooking can actually provide additional sustenance. Cooling down and storing this water ensures that no drop is wasted.

Reducing Water Loss Through Evaporation

In hot, arid climates, evaporation is a significant concern. To prevent water loss, store your water containers in shaded areas or bury them partially underground where the temperature is cooler. If you are using a makeshift water storage system like a bladder or bamboo container, wrap it in cloth or leaves to reduce exposure to sunlight.

When collecting water in ponds or small streams, avoid using open containers. Instead, cover your water storage units with lids or leaves to limit evaporation. If you have access to clay, you can line shallow water collection pits to slow down evaporation and prevent the water from seeping into the ground too quickly.

By understanding how to recycle water, minimize waste, and prevent evaporation, you make the most of the water you have, significantly extending your ability to survive during drought conditions.

BUILDING RAINWATER COLLECTION SYSTEMS

Rainwater is one of the most reliable sources of fresh water in the wilderness, but collecting and storing it efficiently requires careful planning and construction. Building effective rainwater collection systems ensures that you can capture every drop, providing you with a consistent supply of water even when streams or rivers are unavailable.

Choosing the Right Location

Location is critical when building a rainwater collection system. Choose an area with natural runoff, such as below the edge of a large rock, under a cliff, or beneath the canopy of a tree. These areas help funnel water into your collection system more effectively.

If the terrain is relatively flat, you can create a slight slope or build a simple trench that guides water toward your collection point. Additionally, avoid areas near animal trails or where contaminants like leaves or dirt may accumulate and pollute your water supply.

Constructing a Simple Rainwater Catchment System

A basic rainwater catchment system can be made using natural materials such as leaves, bark, or even large stones. Here's how to construct a simple setup:

1. Create a Funnel: Large leaves, like banana or palm leaves, can be arranged to create a natural funnel that directs water into your storage container. Lay them out overlapping each other, ensuring that water flows smoothly from one leaf to the next. If large leaves are not available, use birch bark or pieces of bamboo split in half to create a trough system.
2. Build a Frame: Support the funnel with a frame made from branches or sticks. Arrange the leaves or bark on this frame, ensuring that the water flows downward into your container. Angle the funnel so that water runs efficiently without spilling.
3. Use a Storage Container: At the bottom of the funnel, place your water storage container. This could be a gourd, a hollow bamboo section, or a bark container lined with clay for added waterproofing. Ensure that the container is secure and positioned to catch the maximum amount of water.

This setup works well during light to moderate rainfalls. For heavy rains, consider digging a shallow pit and lining it with clay or stones to create a small reservoir. Cover the reservoir with leaves or a makeshift lid to reduce contamination and evaporation.

Advanced Rainwater Collection Systems

If you have access to larger materials like tarps, ponchos, or sheets of plastic, you can create more advanced rainwater collection systems that significantly increase your water storage capacity. These systems are particularly useful if you anticipate long periods between rainfalls.

1. Tarp Collection System: Set up the tarp as a canopy, stretching it between trees or poles at a slight angle so water flows toward a collection point. The water runs off the tarp and into a container placed at the lowest point. Secure the edges of the tarp tightly to prevent it from blowing away and to ensure that water doesn't leak out.
2. Rock Catchment: Large, flat rocks naturally collect rainwater and can be utilized as part of your system. Place containers beneath the edges of these rocks where water drips off. You can also position leaves or small pieces of bark beneath these points to channel water more effectively into your storage system.
3. Clay Lined Reservoirs: If you're setting up a long-term camp, digging a larger pit and lining it with clay can create a reliable water storage reservoir. The clay prevents water from seeping into the ground. Build a cover from branches and leaves to minimize evaporation and keep debris out.

These advanced systems allow you to collect significant amounts of water during rainfalls, providing a backup supply that can last days or weeks, depending on your usage and the environmental conditions.

PURIFYING COLLECTED WATER

While collecting and storing rainwater is essential, ensuring its safety is equally important. Even rainwater can become contaminated by bird droppings, debris, or pollutants. To purify collected water, there are several methods:

1. Boiling: Boiling is the most effective way to kill bacteria and parasites. If you have the means to create fire, always boil collected water for at least 5-10 minutes before drinking.
2. Solar Purification: In the absence of fire, solar purification can be used. Fill a clear plastic or glass container with water and place it in direct sunlight for at least 6 hours. The UV rays kill many harmful organisms, making the water safer to drink.
3. Filtration: Using materials like sand, charcoal, and gravel, you can build a basic water filter. Layer these materials in a container or a bamboo segment, pour the water through the filter, and collect it in another container. This method removes larger particles and some contaminants, but boiling or solar purification should follow for complete safety.

CONCLUSION

Water storage and conservation are critical skills for wilderness survival, especially when faced with challenges like droughts or limited access to natural water sources. By learning to create water storage systems from natural materials, efficiently use limited water resources, and build rainwater collection systems, you gain the ability to manage and conserve water effectively. These techniques empower you to secure a consistent water supply, ensuring that you remain hydrated and safe regardless of the environmental conditions.

BOOK 31

CREATING CAMP SAFETY SYSTEMS

In the wilderness, ensuring the safety of your camp is crucial for survival. Whether you are alone or with a group, camp security protects against predators, deters intruders, and prevents accidents that could endanger your life. Establishing a secure perimeter, setting up warning systems, and practicing safe fire and food storage methods are all vital components of an effective camp safety system. This chapter delves into each of these aspects, providing detailed techniques and strategies for creating a safe and well-protected camp environment.

ESTABLISHING PERIMETER SECURITY

The first step in securing your camp is to establish a perimeter that serves as a protective barrier. A well-defined perimeter helps keep animals and potential intruders at a distance, while also providing you with an early warning system should anything approach your camp. Establishing a perimeter involves choosing the right location, using natural resources effectively, and creating barriers that deter wildlife and human threats.

Choosing the Right Location for Your Camp

Before establishing a perimeter, the location of your camp is critical. Ideally, your camp should be in an area that is naturally defensible and offers a clear line of sight in multiple directions. Look for spots such as high ground or areas near natural barriers like cliffs, dense vegetation, or rock formations. These natural features can serve as part of your perimeter, reducing the number of areas you need to secure.

Avoid camping too close to animal trails or watering holes, as these locations can attract predators or other animals that may pose a threat. Similarly, be cautious when setting up camp near open fields where visibility is limited, as this can make it difficult to detect approaching dangers.

Defining and Marking the Perimeter

Once you have selected an appropriate campsite, the next step is to clearly define your camp's perimeter. The size of your perimeter will depend on the terrain and the number of people in your group, but it should be large enough to allow safe movement within the camp while keeping potential threats at a manageable distance.

- Using Natural Materials: Gather branches, rocks, and other natural debris to create a visible boundary around your camp. Build a simple fence using long branches or logs, staking them into the ground to create a low barrier. This fence serves as a deterrent for smaller animals and helps mark the area as your territory. For a more substantial barrier, sharpen the ends of the stakes and arrange them facing outward to discourage intruders from approaching.

- Warning Traps and Obstacles: To enhance perimeter security, set up simple traps and obstacles that can alert you if anything tries to cross the boundary. For example, dig small trenches or pits around the perimeter, covering them lightly with branches or leaves. These traps won't necessarily harm larger animals but can be enough to alert you when they are disturbed.

- Trip Lines: Another effective method is to set up trip lines using cordage, vines, or any available rope. String these lines low to the ground between trees or stakes. Attach small noisemakers, such as empty cans or pieces of metal, to the lines so they rattle or clang when the line is tripped. This simple setup acts as an early warning system for both animal and human intruders.

Natural Camouflage and Concealment

In addition to establishing a physical barrier, using camouflage and concealment techniques helps keep your camp safe by making it less visible to threats. To achieve this:

- Blend Your Shelter with the Environment: Use foliage, branches, and earth to camouflage your shelter, making it difficult to spot from a distance. Avoid bright or reflective materials that might catch light and reveal your location.

- Cover High-Traffic Areas: Paths leading in and out of your camp should be concealed to prevent forming visible trails. Lay down leaves, grass, or small branches to mask tracks and maintain a low profile.

These techniques, when combined with a physical perimeter, create multiple layers of security, reducing the likelihood of unwanted encounters and giving you more control over your environment.

SETTING UP WARNING SYSTEMS AND ALARMS

Warning systems and alarms are essential components of a secure camp. They serve as early alerts that allow you to react quickly when potential threats approach, whether those threats come in the form of wildlife, other humans, or environmental dangers. These systems do not need to be complex; simple, effective alarms can be constructed using natural materials and basic tools.

Visual and Audible Alarm Systems

When setting up alarms, aim to create systems that either make noise or provide visual signals to alert you when your camp is breached. Here are a few methods:

1. Can and Stone Alarms: Collect several small, metal cans or hollow pieces of bamboo and fill them with stones or pebbles. Suspend these noisemakers on trip lines around your camp's

perimeter, tying them at head or chest height to catch anything that moves through the area. When the line is tripped, the cans or bamboo will rattle loudly, alerting you to movement.

2. Hanging Signals: Set up visual alarms by hanging pieces of brightly colored cloth or reflective material at the edges of your perimeter. In daylight, these markers can serve as visual cues if they are disturbed or moved. At night, the same markers can reflect light from a campfire or flashlight, signaling that something has brushed against them.

3. Natural Sound Alerts: If you're in a wooded area, use the environment to create sound alerts. Hang dry leaves, pinecones, or other noisy natural materials on lines or branches so they rustle or fall when disturbed. These alerts are subtle but effective, blending naturally with the surroundings while giving you an audible signal of movement.

Animal Deterrent Systems

Deterring animals, particularly large predators like bears or big cats, is an important aspect of camp safety. Creating alarms that target these animals helps protect both your camp and your food supplies:

1. Scent-Based Alarms: In predator-heavy areas, use scent to deter animals from approaching your camp. Collect human hair, pieces of clothing, or other items with a strong human scent and hang them at the edges of your camp. The unfamiliar smell can often deter animals from entering the area.

2. Bear Bells and Wind Chimes: Setting up simple bear bells or makeshift wind chimes made from bones, shells, or metal pieces can create constant noise, which may deter predators. Animals are often wary of unfamiliar sounds, and a camp that emits such noises may be avoided altogether.

3. Firelight as a Deterrent: Animals are naturally wary of fire, and keeping a small fire going at night can help keep predators at bay. However, if you use fire as a deterrent, maintain it safely and at a manageable size to prevent it from becoming a hazard (more on fire safety below).

IMPLEMENTING SAFE FIRE AND FOOD STORAGE PRACTICES

Fire is both an essential tool and a potential hazard in the wilderness. It provides warmth, cooks food, and offers protection against animals, but without proper management, it can become dangerous. Likewise, food storage practices are critical for maintaining safety, as improperly stored food can attract wildlife, increasing the risk of encounters. Properly managing fire and food storage systems is fundamental to keeping your camp safe.

Safe Fire Practices

When setting up and maintaining a fire, safety is the top priority. A well-managed fire provides numerous benefits, but it must be built and maintained with caution to prevent accidents or unwanted attention.

1. Choosing a Fire Site: Select a location for your fire that is protected from wind but not en-

closed by dense foliage, which could catch fire. Ideally, clear an area of about 10 feet around the fire pit, removing any dry leaves, grass, or debris. Dig a shallow pit to contain the fire, and surround it with stones to prevent the flames from spreading.

2. Building a Safe Fire: Use small tinder and kindling to start your fire, and gradually add larger sticks and logs. Avoid building a fire that is too large, as it can become difficult to control. A small, contained fire provides enough heat for cooking and warmth without becoming a hazard.

3. Maintaining and Extinguishing the Fire: Keep water or sand nearby to quickly extinguish the fire if needed. When you're ready to put the fire out, douse it thoroughly with water, ensuring that all embers are cool before leaving the site or going to sleep. Stir the ashes to check for hidden hot spots that could reignite.

By following these practices, you can safely manage fire in your camp, reducing the risk of accidents while still benefiting from its protective and practical uses.

Proper Food Storage Techniques

Food storage is another critical aspect of camp safety, as improperly stored food is one of the primary attractants for wildlife. Ensuring your food is stored in a way that minimizes smells and keeps it out of reach from animals helps protect both your food supplies and your safety.

1. Hanging Food: In predator-heavy areas, hanging food is one of the most effective storage methods. Use a tree with a sturdy branch at least 10-15 feet off the ground and several feet away from the trunk. Place your food in a secure bag (or, if you have one, a bear-proof container) and hoist it up using cordage. Ensure that the bag is high enough to be out of reach of bears and other climbing animals like raccoons.

2. Burying Food Caches: In environments where hanging food isn't feasible, such as arid or treeless regions, burying food caches can be a solution. Dig a hole away from your camp, place your food in a sealed container, and cover it with soil and natural debris. Make sure to bury it deep enough to prevent animals from detecting the scent. Always remember the exact location of your cache to avoid difficulties when retrieving it later.

3. Using Smell-Proof Containers: If available, use smell-proof or airtight containers to minimize the scent of food. Animals, particularly bears, have an extraordinary sense of smell and can detect food from long distances. Sealed containers help reduce this risk, allowing you to store food closer to your camp without attracting predators.

4. Cooking Away from Camp: To further reduce the risk of attracting animals, cook and prepare food at least 100 feet away from your sleeping area. This practice prevents cooking smells from lingering near your shelter and reduces the likelihood of animals associating your camp with food. After cooking, clean all utensils and cooking surfaces thoroughly, and dispose of waste far from your camp to prevent attracting scavengers.

CONCLUSION

Creating camp safety systems is a fundamental aspect of wilderness survival. By establishing a secure perimeter, setting up effective warning systems, and implementing safe fire and food storage practices, you build a protective environment that minimizes threats and keeps you safe. These techniques transform your camp from a temporary resting place into a secure home base, giving you the confidence and stability needed to thrive in the wild. Mastering these safety skills ensures that you can protect yourself, your resources, and any companions, ultimately enhancing your overall survival capabilities.

BOOK 32
ADVANCED FISHING AND AQUATIC SURVIVAL

The wilderness is not only composed of dense forests and sprawling plains; it is also defined by its waterways. Rivers, lakes, and coastal regions offer an abundance of resources—if you know how to harness them. Mastering advanced fishing and aquatic survival techniques opens up a world of opportunities, transforming water from a potential obstacle into a lifeline. In this chapter, we explore the intricate art of creating fish traps and nets from natural materials, the ancient skill of free-diving for underwater hunting, and the construction and use of rafts for navigating rivers and lakes. Each of these skills is a crucial tool in the wilderness, enhancing your ability to gather food, travel, and survive.

CREATING FISH TRAPS AND NETS FROM NATURAL MATERIALS

When you find yourself near a body of water—whether it's a slow-moving river, a tranquil lake, or the rocky shores of a coastal area—setting up fish traps and nets is one of the most effective ways to secure food. Unlike traditional fishing methods that demand time and patience, these techniques work passively, allowing you to tend to other survival tasks while the traps do the work. But, to be effective, you must learn to read the water and understand the behavior of fish.

I remember the first time I saw a funnel trap in action. It was during a trek through the dense forest of the Pacific Northwest. The river we had camped beside was clear and cool, with its current gentle enough to allow fish to swim up against it. The man leading our group, a seasoned survivalist, pointed out how the narrow parts of the river created natural funnels where fish tended to gather. He explained that these bottlenecks were the perfect places to set up traps.

We began by gathering flexible branches from nearby willow trees and lengths of strong, vine-like plants to serve as binding material. The idea was simple but brilliant: create a cylindrical frame using the thick branches, then weave thinner branches to form walls that would trap the fish. The funnel's entrance was wide, guiding fish into the cylinder as they swam upstream, but the interior narrowed, preventing them from finding their way back out. Once set, we anchored the trap using large stones, ensuring it remained stable in the river's current.

By the next morning, our trap had captured a bounty of small trout, their silver bodies shimmering in the morning light. The passive nature of the trap allowed us to focus on other tasks, like gathering firewood and building shelter. This method is a testament to how using the environment to your advantage can yield rewards without constant effort.

The beauty of fish traps is their simplicity and adaptability. You can set them up in various environments, adjusting the materials and structure based on what you find. In lakes, for example, traps can be placed near underwater plants or rock formations where fish seek refuge. Coastal areas, too, offer opportunities—by placing traps in tidal zones, you can catch fish as they move in and out with the tides.

Nets, on the other hand, require a bit more craftsmanship but can yield even greater rewards. I learned to weave a basic drag net from long grasses and reeds. The process involves creating a grid pattern by interlacing strips of fiber, tying each intersection securely to form a web that, when dragged through shallow water, traps fish in its mesh. With practice, the act of weaving becomes rhythmic, and each knot ties you closer to the environment, blending ancient skills with the immediate needs of survival. Nets can also be set up as stationary barriers, left in place overnight to catch fish as they swim.

FREE-DIVING TECHNIQUES FOR AQUATIC HUNTING

Sometimes, passive fishing methods aren't enough. In environments where fish are scarce or elusive, or when you need a quick meal, direct action is necessary. This is where free-diving becomes an invaluable skill. Diving beneath the water's surface to hunt fish, gather shellfish, or harvest underwater plants demands both physical and mental discipline. It's a practice rooted in ancient traditions, requiring breath control, patience, and the ability to move silently through the water.

The first time I attempted free-diving for food, I felt a mix of excitement and anxiety. We were camped along a deep, crystal-clear lake in the foothills of a mountain range. The water was so transparent that, even from the surface, I could see fish darting among the submerged logs and rocks below. Our guide, an experienced diver, walked us through the essentials of breath control and the proper way to enter the water without causing a splash that would send the fish scattering.

Free-diving is as much about preparation as it is about action. We practiced breath-hold exercises on the shore first—learning how to inhale deeply, expanding the lungs, and exhaling slowly to extend our breath capacity. The key, he said, was to stay calm, to slow your heart rate, and to let your body adjust to the deprivation of oxygen without panic. I remember lying on my back, watching the sky, as I held my breath for longer and longer periods, my body gradually accepting the rhythm.

When it was time to dive, the cold shock of the water was jarring, but I pushed through, focusing on staying calm. Underwater, the world became a realm of muted sounds and cool, fluid motion. Fish hovered in the shadows, moving leisurely until they sensed my presence. I held my spear—a simple wooden shaft I had carved and fire-hardened—and waited, letting the fish become accustomed to my presence. It was a game of patience. When a trout swam close enough, I lunged forward, aiming slightly below the fish to account for the refraction of light through water.

The strike was clean. As I surfaced, holding my catch, I felt a surge of triumph. Hunting underwater demands control and skill, but the rewards are immediate and deeply satisfying.

Free-diving isn't just about hunting fish; it's also a way to gather shellfish and edible aquatic plants, expanding your food sources significantly.

BUILDING AND USING RAFTS FOR RIVER AND LAKE SURVIVAL

Waterways are not only sources of food but also natural highways through the wilderness. Rivers and lakes can provide efficient routes for traveling great distances, avoiding dense forest paths or rugged mountain terrain. However, navigating these bodies of water requires the ability to build and use rafts effectively. Constructing a raft from natural materials allows you to move efficiently across lakes or down rivers, transforming what could be an obstacle into a strategic advantage.

Building a raft begins with understanding the local resources. On one occasion, while navigating a long stretch of river through the lowlands, we decided to construct a raft. We gathered logs from fallen trees—light but sturdy wood like spruce or pine. The key was finding logs of similar size and buoyancy. We lashed them together using vines and flexible green branches. To reinforce the structure, we added crossbeams, securing them tightly to prevent the raft from coming apart in the current.

Once we launched the raft into the river, it floated easily, its surface stable enough to support our gear and ourselves. The first thing I noticed was how freeing it felt to glide along the river's surface, propelled by the current. Using long poles cut from saplings, we steered the raft, pushing against the riverbed to navigate around rocks and shallows. The raft was more than just transportation; it was a mobile base, allowing us to fish from its platform and gather supplies along the banks without having to constantly set up and break down camp.

The versatility of a raft cannot be overstated. On lakes, it serves as a fishing platform, enabling you to cast nets or lines into deeper waters where fish are more plentiful. On rivers, it allows you to travel quickly, covering distances that would take days to hike through thick brush or rugged terrain. However, it's essential to know the river's patterns—the flow speed, the location of rapids, and the depth of the water. Navigating rapids can be dangerous, requiring quick decision-making and the ability to read the river's currents.

Raft building also serves another purpose: a temporary escape route. If an area becomes unsafe due to predators or the approach of other humans, a raft offers a way to quickly relocate, carrying your supplies with you. It is a movable sanctuary in an environment that can shift unpredictably.

CONCLUSION

Advanced fishing and aquatic survival techniques are indispensable for anyone seeking to live off the land. By mastering the skills of building fish traps and nets, free-diving for underwater resources, and constructing rafts, you turn water from a barrier into a vital resource. These techniques allow you to sustain yourself, navigate efficiently, and access parts of the wilderness that would otherwise remain unreachable. Waterways become both a source of sustenance and a path forward, transforming the way you interact with the wilderness and enhancing your ability to survive and thrive.

BOOK 33
HANDLING INJURIES IN THE WILDERNESS

In the wilderness, even the smallest injury can escalate into a serious threat if not handled properly. When you're far from civilization, with no immediate access to a hospital or modern medical facilities, knowing how to manage wounds, fractures, and other emergencies becomes a matter of life and death. I've seen firsthand how a small mistake—a misstep on a rocky trail or a careless slip with a knife—can lead to situations that require swift, decisive action. The key to survival is not just knowing the skills but also staying calm under pressure. In this chapter, we'll explore how to treat common wilderness injuries using natural remedies, build an improvised first aid kit, and manage severe emergencies when medical help is out of reach.

TREATING COMMON WILDERNESS INJURIES WITH NATURAL REMEDIES

The wilderness is full of hazards—sharp rocks, thorny underbrush, venomous creatures. It's inevitable that, at some point, you'll suffer cuts, scrapes, or insect bites. Knowing how to use the resources around you to treat these injuries can prevent them from becoming more serious.

The Art of Treating Cuts and Scrapes

I remember the time I was hiking through dense forest, the kind where sunlight barely touches the ground, and every step is a careful maneuver around roots and fallen branches. A sharp, jagged stone caught my boot, and before I knew it, I'd stumbled and scraped my forearm against a broken branch. The cut wasn't deep, but it bled freely, and I knew that in the wilderness, even a small wound could turn dangerous if it became infected.

The first step is always to clean the wound. If you're lucky enough to have a source of clean water nearby—a river or stream—you rinse the area thoroughly, letting the cool water flush out dirt and debris. But sometimes, clean water isn't an option. In these cases, I've learned to use a simple antiseptic solution made from pine resin. The sticky sap, found oozing from pine trees, has natural antibacterial properties. I remember warming it over a fire until it dissolved into a liquid, then mixing it with cooled, boiled water. Applying this resin wash to the wound felt like tapping into the wisdom of those who lived off the land for centuries.

After cleaning the wound, the next step is protection. Without a modern bandage, I turned to plantain leaves, a plant I'd learned about from an old survival guide. It grows low to the ground and, when crushed, releases a soothing juice. I crushed several leaves, spread the pulp over the wound, and secured it with a strip of cloth from my shirt. The plantain not only helped the wound heal but also reduced the pain and swelling. Nature, I realized, has a way of providing exactly what we need, as long as we know where to look.

Dealing with Burns in the Wilderness

Fire is an essential tool, but it's also a danger. One evening, while tending a campfire, I accidentally brushed my hand against a hot stone. The burn was immediate—a sharp, searing pain that shot through my fingers. In that moment, I knew that cooling the burn was the priority.

I plunged my hand into the cold water of the nearby stream, feeling the relief as the heat dissipated. But what if water isn't available? In drier environments, I've learned to use mud or clay as an alternative. Smearing a layer of cool mud over the burn can draw out the heat and protect the skin until a better solution is available. Once the area was cooled, I searched for aloe vera, which grows in abundance in some regions. Breaking open a leaf and applying the gel felt like finding a treasure—its soothing properties calmed the burn and promoted healing.

In the absence of aloe, I've also used comfrey leaves. Crushing the leaves to release their juice, I applied it to the burn, knowing that comfrey's natural compounds could help regenerate skin cells and reduce inflammation. In the wilderness, plants like these become lifesavers, turning a painful injury into something manageable.

Insect Bites and Stings: Nature's Irritations

One night, as I lay by the campfire, I felt the sharp sting of a mosquito bite. In the wilderness, insect bites are more than a nuisance—they can lead to infections or allergic reactions if not treated. I remembered what an old friend, a wilderness guide, had once told me: plantain leaves are your best friend for stings and bites. I found a patch nearby, crushed the leaves, and rubbed the paste over the bite. The relief was almost immediate.

Another time, I stumbled into a patch of nettles. My skin erupted in itchy, red welts. I knew I had to find something to soothe the irritation. This time, it was dandelion sap that came to my aid. Pulling up the plant, I broke the stem and applied the milky sap directly to my skin. It wasn't an instant cure, but it took the edge off the itching, enough for me to carry on with setting up camp.

The trick is to know the plants in your environment and how to use them. The wilderness offers many remedies, but they must be applied correctly and with care.

BUILDING AN IMPROVISED FIRST AID KIT

In an ideal world, we'd all carry fully stocked first aid kits. But when you're living off the land or caught unprepared, you have to build your own from what's available. It's a matter of creativity and knowledge—understanding what you need and how to make it with what you have.

Bandages and Dressings from Nature

One of the most basic components of any first aid kit is bandages. In the wilderness, I've used large leaves like burdock or mullein to cover wounds. These leaves are soft and broad, perfect for wrapping around cuts or scrapes. If you can find willow bark, you can strip it into long, flexible pieces and use it to secure the leaves in place. I remember one night, deep in the woods, when a companion sliced his hand while preparing wood for a shelter. We wrapped the wound with burdock leaves and secured it with willow bark strips. It was a simple but effective solution, and it kept the wound clean until we could find better supplies.

Natural Antiseptics and Pain Relief

An essential part of any kit is an antiseptic. I've learned to rely on pine resin, which can be collected from pine trees. Melted and mixed with water, it becomes a potent wash for wounds. Another option is charcoal, which can be ground into a powder and mixed with water to create a poultice. I've used this mixture to draw out toxins from infected wounds or insect stings.

For pain relief, nature provides options too. I've often boiled willow bark, which contains salicin, a natural compound similar to aspirin. I recall drinking this bitter tea when a persistent headache threatened to ruin a long hike. The relief was slow but steady, a reminder of how people once relied on the forest for medicine.

HANDLING SEVERE EMERGENCIES WHEN MEDICAL HELP IS UNAVAILABLE

The real test of wilderness survival is not handling small scrapes or bites but managing severe emergencies—broken bones, severe bleeding, or even snakebites. When you're hours or days from help, quick thinking and resourcefulness become your greatest allies.

Managing Broken Bones and Fractures

I once found myself deep in the backcountry when a member of our group slipped on a wet rock and broke his leg. The snap of the bone was a sound I won't forget. In that moment, everything became about stabilization. We used straight branches to create a splint, padding them with moss and strips of cloth to immobilize the leg. It wasn't elegant, but it held firm, and that was all that mattered. We used vines to secure the splint, tying them tightly but not so tight as to cut off circulation.

Creating a makeshift stretcher, we carried him to a more sheltered area. In those moments, every piece of knowledge—from building splints to creating supports—became crucial. It reminded me that improvisation, coupled with basic medical skills, is often all that stands between survival and danger in such situations.

Controlling Severe Bleeding

Severe bleeding is one of the most dangerous scenarios you can face. I've seen how fast blood can flow from a wound, and it's frightening. On one occasion, a deep gash needed immediate attention. We applied pressure using a clean cloth, but it wasn't enough. I knew from experience that a tourniquet might be necessary. Using a strip of vine and a sturdy stick, we tied it above the wound, twisting until the bleeding slowed. It was a last resort, and I monitored closely, loosening it every few minutes to avoid further damage.

Dealing with Snakebites

Snakebites are a terrifying reality in some regions. I remember an encounter with a rattlesnake bite. The person bitten tried to move quickly, but that only made the venom spread faster. The key was to keep calm and still, to reduce the heart rate and slow the venom's travel. We used a charcoal poultice, placing it over the bite to draw out the toxins. It wasn't a cure, but it bought time—time to stabilize and plan our next steps.

CONCLUSION

Handling injuries in the wilderness is about preparation, knowledge, and a calm mind. From treating small scrapes with leaves and sap to managing severe injuries with improvised tools, every skill is a piece of a larger puzzle that ensures survival. The wilderness is both a teacher and a test, and with the right mindset and skills, it becomes a place where even injuries, serious as they may be, can be managed with confidence.

BOOK 34
FOOD PRESERVATION AND STORAGE

When you're out in the wilderness, the ability to store and preserve food is essential. Finding food is only the beginning; keeping it safe and edible over time requires skill and knowledge. I learned this the hard way during my early expeditions, where despite catching enough fish or finding edible plants, I often faced spoilage or lost supplies to wildlife. It became clear that if I was going to survive—and thrive—out in the wild, I needed to master the art of food preservation and storage. This chapter covers some of the most effective methods I've relied on: smoking and drying meat, fermenting and pickling wild foods, and securing supplies from the ever-present threat of wildlife. These skills not only sustain you but also provide a sense of security, knowing that your efforts to find food won't go to waste.

SMOKING AND DRYING MEAT FOR LONG-TERM STORAGE

One of the first skills I honed in the wilderness was the art of preserving meat through smoking and drying. There's nothing like the satisfaction of catching a fish or bringing down a deer, but the thrill quickly fades if you can't keep the meat from spoiling. Without refrigeration, smoking and drying are age-old techniques that transform fresh meat into a long-lasting resource.

The Ritual of Smoking Meat

The first time I smoked meat, I was deep in the forests of the Adirondacks. It was a chilly autumn evening, and the air was crisp, the perfect conditions for a smoking fire. I had managed to catch a trout earlier that day and knew I needed to act fast. The process of smoking is all about patience, and I set up my camp with the intention of staying put for a while.

Setting Up the Smoking Rack

I gathered long green branches from nearby trees, as these are less likely to catch fire. I shaped them into a simple tripod over the fire pit, leaving enough space to hang the fish above the flames. Green wood is essential because it holds its shape and resists burning, making it perfect for building a frame that can withstand hours of exposure to smoke.

The Right Fire for Smoking

I didn't want a roaring flame; I needed a slow, steady smolder. To achieve this, I collected damp moss and wood, stacking it carefully to produce thick, fragrant smoke. It's a balancing act—

enough heat to dry the meat but not so much that it cooks too quickly or chars. The smoke rolled over the fish, which I had sliced into thin fillets. The smell was intoxicating, a mixture of earth and fire that brought a sense of accomplishment. As the hours passed, the fish gradually changed color, turning from fresh pink to a rich, smoky brown. I knew that, if done correctly, this fish could sustain me for days, even weeks.

By the next morning, the trout was dry to the touch but still flexible, the sign of properly smoked meat. Packed carefully into a cloth pouch, it became my sustenance as I traveled further into the wilderness. That trout wasn't just food; it was a lesson in how patience, preparation, and technique come together in the wild.

Drying Meat Under the Sun

Drying meat is another method that's saved me countless times, especially when I've been in areas where firewood is scarce or the weather is hot and dry. I remember one journey through the high desert of Utah, where the sun was relentless, and wood for fires was hard to find. I had caught a rabbit, and the best option was to use the sun to my advantage.

Finding the Right Spot

To dry meat in the sun, you need a place that gets plenty of sunlight and good airflow, but that's also protected from insects and scavengers. I found a rocky outcrop, flat enough to set up a drying frame and high enough to be out of reach for most animals. I cut the meat into thin strips and rubbed them with salt—if you're lucky enough to have some on hand, salt is invaluable, drawing out moisture and acting as a preservative.

Using the Elements

I laid the strips across a makeshift frame made of sagebrush branches. The sun and wind worked together, slowly drawing the moisture out of the meat. Every few hours, I turned the strips, making sure they dried evenly. The process took the entire day and required constant attention to keep flies away, but by sunset, the meat was ready. Dried meat, known as jerky, becomes tough but lightweight and can be carried for weeks, providing critical protein when other food sources are scarce.

FERMENTING AND PICKLING WILD FOODS

While preserving meat is crucial, plants, fruits, and vegetables also need to be stored for the long haul. I learned the art of fermenting and pickling from an old friend who spent years living off the land in the Pacific Northwest. We were in a valley filled with wild onions, dandelion greens, and other edible plants, but we knew these fresh resources wouldn't last long. Fermentation became our solution.

The Magic of Fermentation

Fermenting food is an ancient practice that not only preserves but also enhances its nutritional value. It was late summer when I tried it for the first time. We collected wild cabbage, which is abundant and perfect for fermenting. The leaves were tough, but they held up well during the process.

Creating a Fermentation Brine

Without access to refined salt, we used ash from the campfire, mixing it with boiled water to create a brine. Ash contains minerals that act as a substitute for salt, making it an effective, if unconventional, preservative. We packed the cabbage leaves into a hollowed-out gourd, filling it with the brine to cover the leaves completely. Keeping the vegetables submerged is crucial; exposure to air can lead to spoilage.

The Wait and the Transformation

Fermentation is a waiting game. The gourd stayed in a cool, shaded spot, where we checked it daily. Within a week, the cabbage had transformed, developing the sour, tangy smell typical of fermented foods. It might sound strange, but that smell was a sign of success. Fermented vegetables not only last longer but provide beneficial bacteria that aid digestion and keep the immune system strong—an advantage when you're living off limited resources.

Pickling Wild Berries and Fruits

Pickling is another technique that I've found invaluable, particularly in regions rich with berries and fruits. I recall one trip in the Appalachian Mountains during autumn, where wild crabapples were abundant. Their tartness made them perfect for pickling, but without vinegar, I had to get creative.

Making Vinegar from Scratch

We used the scraps from the crabapples, placing them in a large hollow log filled with water. The natural yeast from the fruit slowly fermented the sugars into vinegar over several weeks. It was a slow process, but patience is the key in the wilderness. When the vinegar was ready, I packed the crabapples into jars made from clay and poured the homemade vinegar over them. I added wild herbs like thyme for flavor. This simple act of preservation meant I had a steady source of vitamin-rich food long after the fresh fruits were gone.

STORING AND PROTECTING SUPPLIES FROM WILDLIFE

Even after preserving food, the challenge of keeping it safe from wildlife remains. Bears, raccoons, and rodents are always on the lookout for an easy meal, and they have no qualms about raiding your supplies. Learning to store food properly and protect it from these opportunistic animals is as critical as the preservation process itself.

Hanging Supplies High in Trees

One of the first things I learned was to hang food from trees. It's a classic technique but effective, especially in dense forests. I remember one night in a remote part of the Cascades when I was woken up by the sound of rustling outside my shelter. A raccoon had found its way to my camp and was sniffing around for a meal. I quickly grabbed my food bag, tied it up, and hoisted it onto a high branch.

Choosing the Right Spot

The key is finding a branch at least 10 feet off the ground and far enough from the trunk so animals like raccoons can't climb out to reach it. I used strong vines to secure the bag, ensuring it wouldn't fall if the branch swayed or if an animal tried to jump for it.

Burying Supplies as a Last Resort

In environments without trees, such as deserts or open plains, I've had to bury my food to keep it safe. During one trek through the prairie, I caught several rabbits and knew that if I didn't hide them, I'd lose everything to coyotes or other scavengers.

Digging a Food Cache

I dug a deep hole, far enough from my camp to avoid attracting animals to my shelter. I lined it with stones to create a barrier and packed the food in, covering it with a thick layer of dirt and rocks. I marked the spot subtly, so I could find it again without drawing attention to it. This method isn't foolproof, but it often buys you enough time to keep moving or find a better storage solution.

CONCLUSION

Food preservation and storage are not just skills—they are the foundation of long-term survival. By learning to smoke and dry meat, ferment and pickle wild foods, and protect supplies from wildlife, you gain control over your resources and security in the wilderness. These methods transform the food you find into a dependable supply that can sustain you for weeks, or even months, ensuring that you're not just surviving but thriving in nature's vast, unpredictable landscape.

BOOK 35

BUILDING LONG-TERM SETTLEMENTS

When it comes to wilderness survival, being able to build and maintain a long-term settlement is a game changer. While temporary camps serve their purpose, especially when you're on the move or in an emergency situation, constructing a semi-permanent campsite provides a level of comfort, stability, and safety that's essential for long-term survival. This chapter focuses on building infrastructure for a long-term wilderness home, covering everything from constructing semi-permanent campsites to developing the infrastructure needed for sustained living, and finally, how to maintain a self-sufficient and sustainable wilderness homestead. These skills are crucial if you ever find yourself needing to create a base camp that can support you for months or even years.

CONSTRUCTING SEMI-PERMANENT CAMPSITES

The transition from a temporary camp to a semi-permanent settlement begins with site selection and strategic planning. It's more than just finding a convenient spot for a night; it's about creating a place that will offer security, resources, and comfort for an extended period. The first time I built a semi-permanent camp was in a forested area of the northern Rockies, and the lessons I learned have stayed with me ever since.

Choosing the Right Location

The first and most crucial step in building a long-term settlement is choosing the right location. Ideally, you want a spot that offers natural protection, access to fresh water, and abundant resources. The location should also be defensible and hidden from both predators and potential human threats. In the northern Rockies, I found a small clearing nestled between two hills, providing natural windbreaks and concealment. The spot was near a stream for water and surrounded by trees, which offered building materials and firewood.

1. Proximity to Water

Water is life. Having a reliable water source nearby—such as a stream, lake, or spring—is essential for drinking, cooking, and cleaning. When choosing a site, I always make sure to be within a short walk of fresh water, but not too close; placing a camp right on the water's edge invites problems with flooding, wildlife, and exposure. About 200 feet from the water's edge is a safe distance, giving you access while keeping hazards at bay.

2. Access to Resources

Building a long-term camp requires a range of natural resources, from wood for building and firewood to stones for constructing foundations or walls. Make sure your chosen location has abundant and diverse resources within a reasonable distance. When I set up my camp in the Rockies, the surrounding forest provided me with an ample supply of timber and plant materials, while the rocky outcrops nearby offered stones for building. A sustainable site is one where you don't have to travel far for your daily needs.

3. Defensibility and Shelter

The wilderness is home to many threats, from predators like bears to harsh weather conditions. Setting up camp near natural barriers, such as rock formations or dense tree lines, provides additional protection. In my experience, positioning your camp against a hillside or beneath a rock outcrop offers natural windbreaks and protection from rain. It also reduces visibility from potential intruders, keeping your settlement safer.

Building the Shelter: Semi-Permanent Structures

Once the location is chosen, it's time to build a shelter that can withstand the elements for months or even years. A semi-permanent shelter requires more than a simple lean-to; it needs to be robust and durable. In my camp, I constructed a log frame shelter, which became my base of operations.

1. Creating the Frame

Using the timber around me, I cut down trees of similar size to form the structure's frame. Green logs work best because they are less prone to splitting. I shaped the logs into a simple rectangular frame, interlocking them at the corners. The design resembled a small cabin but with open sides, allowing for ventilation and visibility.

2. Insulating and Weatherproofing

A semi-permanent shelter must be able to handle rain, wind, and cold. I filled the gaps between the logs with mud, clay, and moss, creating a natural sealant that dried to form an insulating layer. For the roof, I used large bark sheets from fallen trees, overlapping them like shingles and tying them down with vines to keep them secure during storms.

3. Adding Comfort Features

In a long-term camp, comfort becomes crucial. I added a raised platform inside the shelter for sleeping, made from smaller logs lashed together and covered with a thick layer of pine boughs. This kept me off the cold ground and away from insects. As the camp developed, I built a simple fire pit outside the entrance, ensuring it was close enough to provide warmth but far enough to prevent smoke from filling the shelter.

BUILDING INFRASTRUCTURE FOR LONG-TERM SURVIVAL

Once the shelter is established, the next step is to develop the infrastructure needed to support a long-term settlement. This includes building facilities for cooking, food storage, water collection, and waste management. These systems transform a campsite into a self-sustaining home.

Building a Cooking Area and Fire Pit

Cooking over an open flame is one of the great pleasures of wilderness living, but it requires a safe and efficient setup. I built a stone-lined fire pit a few feet from my shelter. The stones not only contained the fire but also absorbed and radiated heat, making cooking more efficient and keeping the area warm even after the flames died down.

1. Constructing a Cooking Frame

Over the fire pit, I erected a tripod structure using sturdy branches. I tied these together at the top, creating a stable frame from which to hang a pot or grill food. Having a cooking area set up like this allows for flexibility—whether I'm boiling water, grilling fish, or smoking meat, I can adjust the setup easily.

2. Building a Smokehouse

One of the most important structures I added was a small smokehouse. Using stones and mud, I built a chimney-like structure next to the fire pit, allowing me to hang and smoke meat for long-term storage. The smokehouse kept the meat away from animals and insects, while the slow, consistent heat ensured thorough drying and preservation.

Water Collection and Filtration

In addition to having a nearby water source, it's essential to develop systems for collecting and filtering water. I set up rain catchment systems using large leaves and bark sheets tied to a frame. Positioned to funnel water into a clay pot, this simple system provided me with fresh rainwater even during dry spells.

For filtration, I built a basic filter using layers of sand, charcoal, and gravel placed inside a hollowed log. When water from the stream or rain catchment system was poured through, it was cleaned of debris and bacteria, making it safe to drink. Maintaining access to clean water is one of the most critical aspects of a long-term settlement, as it supports not only hydration but also cooking, cleaning, and hygiene.

Food Storage Systems

A long-term camp requires effective food storage to keep supplies safe from animals and rot. I constructed elevated platforms to store my food supplies. These platforms, raised high on poles and accessed by a ladder, kept my food out of reach from wildlife such as bears and raccoons. I lined the storage containers with pine needles and ash to mask food odors and deter animals further.

MAINTAINING A SELF-SUFFICIENT, SUSTAINABLE WILDERNESS HOME

Building a settlement is only the beginning; maintaining it sustainably is what ensures long-term survival. This involves not only keeping structures in good repair but also developing systems that provide food, water, and energy without depleting the surrounding environment.

Developing a Garden

Growing food in the wilderness is a key component of self-sufficiency. I found a sunny patch of land close to my shelter and cleared it for a small garden. Using hand-dug irrigation channels from the nearby stream, I was able to water the crops. I planted hardy, wild edibles like wild onions, dandelion greens, and yarrow, as well as seeds I had brought with me for more familiar crops like beans and squash.

Gardening in the wilderness takes patience and a deep understanding of the soil and weather patterns. I used natural mulch from the forest floor to enrich the soil and maintain moisture. Over time, the garden became a reliable source of fresh greens, complementing the fish, game, and foraged foods I relied on.

Renewable Energy Sources

In the wilderness, every resource must be used carefully, and firewood is no exception. To conserve wood, I built a solar oven using stones and a reflective surface made from a polished piece of metal I had scavenged. The solar oven, placed in a sunny spot, allowed me to cook food without using precious firewood during daylight hours.

Additionally, I set up a small waterwheel in the nearby stream. This simple device harnessed the stream's energy to grind grains and nuts or power basic tools I fashioned. Renewable energy systems like these extend your resources, ensuring that you're not overusing or exhausting the natural environment around you.

Maintaining the Camp and Structures

In a long-term settlement, routine maintenance is crucial. I made it a habit to inspect the shelter and other structures regularly, repairing any damage caused by weather or wildlife. Using mud and clay, I patched cracks in the walls of my shelter, and I checked the roof after storms to replace any displaced bark sheets.

Waste management is another critical aspect. I dug composting pits far from the water source to manage organic waste, turning it into fertilizer for the garden. Proper waste disposal not only keeps the camp clean but also prevents attracting animals.

CONCLUSION

Building a long-term settlement in the wilderness is about creating a home that supports life sustainably. From constructing a secure shelter to developing infrastructure for food, water, and energy, these skills are essential for turning the wilderness into a place where you can not only survive but truly thrive. By using natural resources wisely and maintaining your camp with care, you establish a self-sufficient and sustainable wilderness home, transforming the forest, the mountain, or the desert into a place where you can live in harmony with nature for as long as needed.Conclusion

Wilderness survival is not just about learning a set of skills; it's a comprehensive way of life that demands dedication, adaptability, and a profound respect for nature. It transforms your relationship with the natural world, pushing you to develop resilience, patience, and resourcefulness. As we wrap up this guide, it's important to reflect on the journey you've embarked upon and how these skills, when practiced with consistency and commitment, build a foundation for long-term survival and a deeper connection with the wilderness.

Reflections on Long-Term Wilderness Survival are essential to understand the transformation you experience when living off the land. The wilderness is an environment of constant change, where the challenges you face are both physical and psychological. It's a place that tests your endurance, adaptability, and problem-solving abilities every day. When I recall my own experiences, I am reminded of the solitude that comes with life in the wild. There were long nights when the only sounds were those of the wind and nocturnal animals, and it was in these moments that I learned the true meaning of being alone with oneself. This solitude, however daunting it may seem, is a gift. It forces you to confront your fears and doubts, helping you grow stronger mentally and emotionally.

Every skill you learn in the wilderness is intertwined with the next. Whether it's building shelters, purifying water, or foraging for food, each aspect of survival connects to create a sustainable way of living. These skills aren't isolated tasks; they are part of a larger system that ensures your long-term survival. The more you practice, the more you understand the ecosystem you are part of, and you begin to recognize the rhythms of nature—the way weather patterns shift, how animals behave, and the growth cycles of plants. You become attuned to the subtle cues that tell you when rain is coming or where to find water. This heightened awareness is one of the greatest gifts that the wilderness offers, teaching you to read and respond to the environment as if it were an extension of yourself.

However, survival isn't just about observation and reaction; it's also about mindset. Staying committed to self-sufficiency and sustainability is the backbone of wilderness survival. Self-sufficiency means more than just being able to hunt, gather, or build; it means cultivating a mindset that prioritizes conservation and sustainable living. You quickly learn that the resources around you are limited, and they must be used wisely. Over time, you understand that the key to surviving in the long term is to take only what you need and ensure that the environment can regenerate. This is why practices like rotating foraging locations and preserving food through techniques like smoking or fermenting are crucial. They allow you to minimize impact and maintain a balance with nature, ensuring that your resources remain available not just for days but for months or even years.

When I set up long-term camps, I always plan for sustainability. I make sure that my water sources are clean and regularly filtered, that the firewood I gather is from deadfall rather than living trees, and that my garden patches rotate with each season. It's about finding a rhythm where the environment and your needs coexist harmoniously. It's not just survival; it's living in harmony with the land. This approach goes beyond basic survival instincts—it becomes a philosophy, one that extends to every part of the wilderness experience.

The wilderness has a way of teaching humility. There are times when your skills will be tested, and even the most prepared individual can find themselves facing unforeseen challenges. Storms can destroy shelters, predators can raid food stores, and injuries can happen when least expected. It is in these moments that you must rely on the foundation you've built—both the physical skills and the mental resilience you've honed. Staying committed means persisting through setbacks, learning from each mistake, and adapting. It's about keeping a calm and measured approach when things don't go as planned, knowing that you have the tools and knowledge to find a solution.

The Journey Beyond is where the true depth of wilderness survival begins. Mastering these skills is not an end but a continuous process of growth and learning. The wilderness is vast, and each environment—whether forest, desert, mountain, or coastal area—presents new challenges and opportunities. To truly excel, you must remain a lifelong student of nature. This means continuing to refine your skills, exploring new techniques, and adapting what you know to different terrains and climates. For every success you have, there will be new tests that push you to expand your knowledge and capabilities.

In my years of wilderness exploration, I've learned that the journey never really ends. The moment you feel you've mastered something, nature finds a way to remind you of its complexity. This is why ongoing practice and skill development are essential. For example, tracking and navigation techniques that work in dense forests might not apply in deserts or open plains, where the landscape offers fewer landmarks. Building shelters in one environment may require different materials and methods in another. Every new experience adds to your understanding, making you a more versatile and adaptable survivor.

The beauty of continuing your wilderness journey is that it enriches your life beyond survival. It brings you closer to the natural world, turning the wilderness into a place of refuge rather than a threat. You begin to appreciate the small details—the way a stream flows, the calls of birds, the changing colors of the leaves. These experiences build a relationship with the land that goes deeper than mere survival. You start to see the wilderness as a partner, one that offers as much as it demands.

And it's not just about the wilderness; it's about what you bring back with you. The skills you develop and the resilience you build can be carried into other parts of your life. The patience you learn while waiting for a fish to bite, the problem-solving skills you employ when constructing a shelter, and the ability to adapt to changing conditions—all these elements shape your character, making you more capable, more confident, and more connected to the world around you.

THE WILDERNESS BEYOND SURVIVAL

Ultimately, this guide is just the beginning. The wilderness invites you to push your limits, to become more self-reliant, and to embrace the beauty of living simply and sustainably. It's a life-long practice of honing your skills and deepening your understanding. Whether you're setting up a semi-permanent camp or adapting to new terrains, the principles of long-term wilderness survival will always apply, but they will continue to evolve with each experience you gain.

There's a profound satisfaction in knowing you can live off the land, that you have the skills to thrive without relying on modern conveniences. It's a return to a simpler, more connected way of life. The skills covered in this guide—fire-starting, food preservation, foraging, and shelter building—are the building blocks of a life lived in harmony with nature. But beyond the practical aspects, it's the mindset you develop and the lessons you learn from nature that become the true gifts of wilderness survival.

As you move forward, remember that every step taken in the wilderness is an opportunity to grow, learn, and become more attuned to the world around you. The path of the wilderness survivor is one of continuous discovery, and every challenge faced is an invitation to deepen your connection with the land. Stay committed, stay curious, and let the wilderness guide you beyond mere survival into a life that is truly fulfilling.

YOUR EXCLUSIVE BONUS

30-DAY FAMILY SURVIVAL PLAN FROM BEGINNERS TO EXPERTS FAMILY RESILIENCE WORKBOOK

SCAN ME

Made in United States
Troutdale, OR
01/04/2025

27496352R00113